T0246535

STORIES TOLD
THROUGH SOUND

STORIES TOLD THROUGH SOUND

The Craft of Writing Audio Dramas for Podcasts, Streaming, and Radio

BARRY M. PUTT, JR.

Essex, Connecticut

APPLAUSE
THEATRE & CINEMA BOOKS

An imprint of Globe Pequot, the trade division of
The Rowman & Littlefield Publishing Group, Inc.
4501 Forbes Blvd., Ste. 200
Lanham, MD 20706
www.rowman.com

Distributed by NATIONAL BOOK NETWORK

Copyright © 2023 by Barry M. Putt, Jr.

Beyond the Door script adaptation by Barry M. Putt, Jr. of Philip K. Dick's short story originally aired on the audio-drama series *Radio Theater Project*. Script excerpts used with the kind permission of Radio Theater Project.

"The Business Side of Writing with Barry: Introduction to the Personal Career Ladder," by Barry M. Putt, Jr. first appeared in the June 15, 2007 issue of *Riprap Entertainment TV Ezine* published by Riprap Entertainment.

Mysterious Island audio-drama adaptation of Jules Verne's novel by Barry M. Putt, Jr. All rights reserved by the author.

All illustrations are by Letícia Brito (letticeart).
Back cover photo by Mandee K. Hammerstein

All rights reserved. No part of this book may be reproduced in any form or by any electronic or mechanical means, including information storage and retrieval systems, without written permission from the publisher, except by a reviewer who may quote passages in a review.

British Library Cataloguing in Publication Information available

Library of Congress Cataloging-in-Publication Data

Names: Putt, Barry M., Jr., author.
Title: Stories told through sound : the craft of writing audio dramas for
   podcasts, streaming, and radio / Barry M. Putt, Jr.
Description: Essex, Connecticut : Applause, [2024] | Includes
   bibliographical references and index.
Identifiers: LCCN 2023019485 (print) | LCCN 2023019486 (ebook) | ISBN
   9781493065349 (paperback) | ISBN 9781493065356 (epub)
Subjects: LCSH: Radio plays—Technique. | LCGFT: Radio plays.
Classification: LCC PN1991.73 P22 2024 (print) | LCC PN1991.73 (ebook) |
   DDC 791.44/7—dc23/eng/20230502
LC record available at https://lccn.loc.gov/2023019485
LC ebook record available at https://lccn.loc.gov/2023019486

∞™ The paper used in this publication meets the minimum requirements of American National Standard for Information Sciences—Permanence of Paper for Printed Library Materials, ANSI/NISO Z39.48-1992

To all storytellers:
Audio drama is a powerful, abundant, and welcoming frontier.

Contents

Acknowledgments

This book would not have been possible without the help of many people.

My sincere gratitude goes to all audio-drama professionals interviewed for this book whose individual contributions have enriched the medium. They include: Jeffrey Adams (*Icebox Radio Theater*), Robert Arnold (*Spoken Signal Audio Drama*), Lawrence Albert (*Aural Vision, LLC*), David Benedict (*Atlanta Radio Theatre Company*), Ron Butler (*Atlanta Radio Theatre Company*), M.J. Elliott (*Aural Vision, LLC*), Fred Greenhalgh (*Dagaz Media*), Thomas Lopez (*ZBS Foundation*), Joseph C. McGuire (*Radio Theater Project*), William Alan Ritch (*Atlanta Radio Theatre Company*), Jerry Robbins (*Colonial Radio Theatre on the Air*), Steve Rubenstein (*Shoestring Radio Theatre*), Roger Rittner (*Pulp Radio*), Monica Sullivan (*Shoestring Radio Theatre*), Jack Ward (*The Sonic Society*), and Jim Wicker (*The Radio Theatre Project*). I encourage you to check out their work.

I truly appreciate the assistance of Daniel Calandro, electronic resources librarian, and Martin Crabtree, reference and information literacy librarian, at Mercer County Community College, along with Carli Lowe, university archivist, and Nick Szydlowski, scholarly communications and digital scholarship librarian at the Dr. Martin Luther King, Jr. Library, San José State University, for their assistance in locating and retrieving key materials associated with the history of audio drama in the United States that were used in the first chapter of this book.

A special thank-you goes to my aunt, Jill D. Morton, for introducing me to audio drama when I was growing up.

I offer my earnest thanks to the wonderful team at Applause Theatre & Cinema Books including Chris Chappell for his editorial guidance and Laurel

Myers, Barbara Claire, Jessica Thwaite, Christy Phillippe, John Cerullo, and Carol Flannery for their knowledge and support during the publication process.

My gratitude goes to writers Kenneth Gordon, Kerri Kochanski, and Lindsay Levesque-Alam, for their critical insight, which helped in the development of this book.

I extend a heartfelt thank-you to Rachel D. Barrett, a gifted teacher and friend, for her unwavering support of my writing career.

Finally, I would like to thank my parents, Judie and Barry M. Putt, Sr., for their support during the writing of this book.

Introduction

With thousands of outlets worldwide and more being added all the time, audio drama has become a vibrant medium for storytelling. Freed from the budget and casting restrictions that are inherent to stage, screen, and TV, if you can dream it up, it can be produced in audio. From intimate tales to epic space battles or period pieces to large-cast musicals, there are no limits to what can be done because the audience creates the visual world of the story in their mind. In *Stories Told through Sound,* I walk you through the entire audio-drama creation process. The book uses the industry in the United States as a model, yet the concepts discussed apply throughout the world.

Whether you are a first-time writer or a seasoned professional looking for a new outlet for your work, the topics covered here will give you insight into the profession of audio-drama writing in an easy-to-understand manner. We will discuss craft aspects, including ways to turn an idea into a fully realized audio play, adaptation techniques, and how to develop an audio-drama series. We will also explore process and business-related aspects, such as successful approaches to use when co-writing an audio drama, how to develop a solid career plan, and time-management tips that will increase your productivity. Each of these areas is geared toward helping you find a method that works for you.

The "Helpful Hints" sections found within the book are filled with information I gained during my tenure in scripting over fifty adaptations and original audio dramas for companies throughout the United States. These include the top reasons audiences don't connect with a character and how to avoid them, ways to create exciting plot twists, and essential elements that will make your marketing plan dynamic. Also featured are insights from other top-tier professionals. Each of these elements is designed to give you a deeper understanding into what it takes to be successful in the industry.

So, dust off that story idea you've been wanting to develop and join me in *Stories Told through Sound*, where I will help you master the tools of the trade so you can create engaging scripts that can become fully realized productions. In audio drama, everything is possible!

Barry M. Putt, Jr.

October 2023

Chapter 1
Getting Started in Audio-Drama Writing

Over the years, the art of telling dramatic stories through sound has been referred to as radio theater, audio theater, and radio drama. Today it is most commonly referred to as "audio drama." It is a growing medium, but one that is still largely untapped. Its history is filled with innovations, trends, and milestones that can help you understand how to most effectively tell stories in this form. Having this knowledge will give you an edge as you craft audio plays and then submit them to companies.

A Concise History of the Medium

In 1914, the first live performance of a stage play—most likely *In the Vanguard* by Katrina Trask—was broadcast on a radio station in San Jose, California.[1, 2, 3] In that moment, the roots of audio drama first took hold.[4] They grew slowly until February of 1922, when General Electric opened radio station WGY in Schenectady, New York. The WGY Players were formed a few months later. They performed a feature-length production of Eugene Walter's

stage play *The Wolf* over the airwaves on August 3, 1922. A month later, the
station began live, weekly broadcasts of plays, including *The Garden of Allah*
by Robert Hichens and *Get-Rich-Quick Wallingford* and *Seven Keys to Bald-
pate* by George M. Cohan. The success of these productions led other radio
stations to broadcast stage plays as well.[5]

In 1923, WGY launched an audio-drama writing competition to encourage script development specifically for radio. Approximately one hundred
scripts were received. Unfortunately, the one that was selected and produced
was not a hit.[6] This prompted the station's program manager, Fred Smith,
to write an original piece entitled *When Love Wakes*, which aired to a more
favorable response.[7] The first network drama *Billeted* debuted the following
year.[8] Audio-drama programming started to attract more and more listeners over the next few years, which helped to establish it as a viable form of
entertainment.

In 1926, radio networks began to broadcast original dramatic series on
a regular basis. This brought about the first era in audio drama's history, one
that roughly coincided with the Golden Age of radio.[9] Most audio-drama
programs at this time were fifteen-minute anthologies that were performed
live over the air five days a week.[10] It wasn't unusual to listen to four different
programs in a single hour.[11] During this time, the acting/writing team of
Freeman Gosden and Charles Correll produced the first audio-drama sitcom,
Sam 'n' Henry, at WGN in Chicago, Illinois. It was inspired by the comic
strip *The Gumps*. During its successful two-year run, Gosden and Correll
petitioned WGN to record the show so it could be sold to other stations. The
network denied their request, which prompted the acting/writing team to
bring the series to a close.[12]

In 1928, Gosden and Correll approached WMAQ about revamping the
concept for *Sam 'n' Henry* into a new sitcom called *Amos 'n' Andy*. While the
series is considered dated and offensive by today's standards, it was one of the

longest-running audio-drama series of the Golden Age, airing for thirty-two years. It featured a blend of European American and African American actors in a variety of roles. WMAQ greenlit the series and approved Gosden and Correll's request to record it, leading episodes of *Amos 'n' Andy* to be preserved on 78 rpm records. These recordings enabled the first audio-drama syndicate to be born.[13]

In 1930, the Blackett-Sample Hummert advertising agency came up with the concept of the daytime soap opera. The agency represented several manufacturers of soap and other household goods. They were looking for audio programing that was geared toward women, who were the primary consumers of their products. Soap operas dealt with everyday life, which was key to the genre's success. Blackett-Sample Hummert employed writer Robert Hardy Andrews to adapt his newspaper series *The Stolen Husband* into an audio-drama soap opera. The show centered around a young man who strove to get ahead in the world of business with the help of his secretary—and his wife, who eventually discovered a growing relationship between the two.[14] Soon after, writer Irna Phillips created the soap opera *Painted Dreams*. The characters she created for the series quickly grew to be role models of empowerment for female listeners throughout the country. The success of the program led Phillips to become a major player in the genre, originating series such as *Today's Children*, *Right to Happiness*, and *The Guiding Light*, which ultimately transitioned to TV for a fifty-nine-year run.[15]

By 1932, the popularity of audio drama had spread throughout the nation. Work in the medium was so abundant that one staff writer at WWJ in Detroit, Michigan, wrote up to eighteen scripts each week. Increasingly, the film industry was concerned about the competition posed by radio's popularity. All large movie studios except for RCA blocked their talent from appearing on radio, but the ban had little impact on the audio-drama industry.[16]

Around 1933, interest in vaudeville-style entertainment began to wane, leading many performers in the field to transition into radio. This migration helped increase the number of new audio-drama programs that were being produced, including *Dick Tracy*, *Buck Rogers*, *Terry and the Pirates*, and *Hop Harrigan*, all of which were audience favorites adapted from popular comic strips of the era.[17, 18]

In January of 1934, a horror anthology series called *Lights Out* premiered. It quickly became a success and pushed the envelope on what could be depicted in an audio-drama series. At one point, audio dramatist Arch Oboler contributed an episode entitled "Burial Service," which depicted a young girl being buried alive. Listeners were so disturbed by the story that many complained to the network. This led the subject matter of future episodes to be softened.[19]

In the fall of 1934, *Lux Radio Theatre* premiered on NBC. It was sponsored by Lux Soap and featured one-hour audio-drama versions of current movies such as *7th Heaven*, *Little Women*, and later *The Wizard of Oz*. The main cast of each film performed their roles in the radio production.[20] The program, hosted by Cecil B. DeMille for many years, helped film companies promote their latest productions.[21] It became so popular that it spawned copycat series, including *Screen Guild Theater* in 1939 and *Screen Director's Playhouse* in 1949. Despite the competition, *Lux Radio Theatre* outlasted them all.[22]

During the mid-1930s, a wide array of genres took hold of the public's interest, including the sitcom *Fibber McGee and Molly* (1935 to 1959) and its spinoff, *The Great Gildersleeve* (1941 to 1958); detective series, such as *The Shadow* (1937 to 1954), *Mr. Keen, Tracer of Lost Persons* (1937 to 1955), and *The Adventures of Ellery Queen* (1939 to 1948); westerns, including *Death Valley Days* (1930 to 1945), *The Lone Ranger* (1933 to 1956), and *Tom Mix Ralston Straight Shooters* (1939 to 1950); and true-crime stories like

Gang Busters (1936 to 1957) and *Mr. District Attorney* (1939 to 1952).[23, 24] Biographical audio dramas also started to proliferate on the airwaves, attracting young writers like playwright Arthur Miller to work on the anthology series *Columbia Workshop* and *Cavalcade of America*.[25]

In 1938, CBS commissioned Orson Wells and John Houseman to adapt the work that their Broadway repertory company the Mercury Theatre was doing to radio. Their weekly audio-drama series, *The Mercury Theatre on the Air*, featured adaptations of well-known classics.[26] It premiered on July 11, 1938, with a production of *Dracula* and quickly became popular with listeners.[27, 28] An October episode of the program featured an adaptation of H.G. Wells's alien-invasion novel *The War of the Worlds*. The script was set in Grover's Mill, New Jersey, and incorporated a blend of direct-address and dialogue scenes. Listeners throughout the United States thought it was an actual news broadcast. Thousands called newspapers and asked what to do. Some people were so panicked they reported seeing Martians. The production demonstrated the unique power audio drama can have on listeners.[29, 30]

During World War II, American history became a popular subject for audio-drama series. In December of 1941, more than sixty million Americans tuned in to listen to *We Hold These Truths*. The program reinforced the challenges the country had faced in the past and aimed to help unite people.[31] It also spawned shows, including *A Woman of America*, which depicted the achievements of women throughout the country, and *Destination Freedom*, which centered on accomplishments by African Americans, such as Benjamin Banneker, Sojourner Truth, and Booker T. Washington.[32]

As the war came to a close, audio drama's popularity was tested by the emergence of television, which reduced the number of listeners in the audio market.[33] Despite this, several notable audio-drama series debuted to great success, including the sitcoms *The Baby Snooks Show* (1944 to 1951), *Our Miss Brooks* (1948 to 1957), and *My Favorite Husband* (1948 to 1951), which became the inspiration for one of the most popular TV shows of all time, *I Love Lucy*.[34]

During the 1950s, network income from TV ads grew from $57 million to twenty-eight times that, enabling TV to become the dominant form of entertainment across the country. The average time individuals spent listening to radio decreased from four hours a day to two.[35] A growing number of networks started to adapt their audio series for television.[36] For a few years, some programs aired both radio and TV editions of their series.[37] Audio drama's Golden Age came to a close on September 30, 1962, when CBS cancelled the last of its scripted radio shows.[38] The following year, audio dramas from the Golden Age, such as *The Shadow* and *The Adventures of Sherlock Holmes*, went into syndication. Since they were no longer in production, they were considered "old." This prompted programs from the Golden Age to be called "old-time radio."[39]

The Silver Age of audio drama began in the mid-1960s, during a transitional time for the industry. There wasn't much money available, which prompted B-level actors to be hired instead of A-listers, who had been a mainstay during the Golden Age.[40] Producers of the era understood that, in the words of scholar Eleanor Patterson, "radio had become a secondary medium that engendered distracted listening."[41] They took this into account when developing new programs and focused on creating more engaging productions. ABC created the first of these in the anthology series *Theater 5*. It featured faster-paced stories that dealt with subjects including gang culture, suicide, and other topical problems of the day. Episodes frequently concluded without issues being resolved. The series was broadcast in stereo instead of mono, which had been the standard during the Golden Age.[42]

In 1970, Thomas Lopez, a radio administrator, producer, and soundman, started the ZBS Foundation on a donated farm in upstate New York.[43]

The small nonprofit company sought to heighten awareness of the wider world through the production of audio drama.[44] They used this philosophy in their inaugural productions that featured the character of Jack Flanders. In preparation to write the Jack Flanders script *Moon over Morocco*, Lopez visited Morocco and observed the feel of the land and its culture. He recorded sounds there that were used as inspiration for the plot and incorporated into the final production as well. Lopez eventually traveled to jungles in Brazil and various locations in India, Tunisia, Portugal, and Greece, where he recorded sounds that were used in other ZBS productions.[45] The company's creative approach led them to become a pioneer in the medium.[46]

The following year, National Public Radio (NPR) put their series *Earplay* (1971 to 1981) on the air.[47] It featured new scripts by known writers, including Edward Albee, Tom Stoppard, and Arthur Kopit.[48] The show explored life and culture in the United States. Some episodes were so well-received that they were adapted into feature films and stage plays. The program received a Peabody Award for its innovative use of sound.[49]

In 1972, revisions to U.S. copyright law led most audio-drama series from the Golden Age to fall into the public domain. This allowed broadcast and sale of these productions to occur without the need for authorization or payment of royalties. As a result, many radio stations began to air shows from the era, which helped create a new audience for them.[50]

The reemergence of audio drama's popularity led the CBS Radio Drama Network to be formed in 1974. It was used as a vehicle to distribute the anthology series *CBS Radio Mystery Theater* (1974 to 1982).[51] The seven-day-a-week show sold out all available advertising slots within four months of its premiere.[52] Stories centered around the era's social and political issues. The use of "theater" in the title, along with ABC's *Theater 5*, prompted the coinage of the phrase "theater of the mind," which became associated with the medium.[53]

In mid-1974, Byron Lewis and Raymond League, heads of the African American advertising agency Uniworld Group, Inc., were inspired by the resurgence of the audio-drama market to create a new soap opera entitled *Sounds of the City*.[54] Each fifteen-minute episode focused on the modern-day struggles and achievements of African American police officer Calvin Taylor and his family's life in a large city. The series, sponsored by Quaker Oats, premiered on twenty-seven of the one hundred and fifty African American radio stations located in large U.S. cities. Four million listeners tuned in daily, which demonstrated the shows' popularity.[55]

In 1976, the independent company Jim French Productions debuted their detective series *The Adventures of Harry Nile*. The company quickly became a master of the genre and built a solid fan base in the process. They went on to release other long-running series such as *Raffles, the Gentleman Thief* and *Murder and the Murdochs*. Jim French Productions holds the distinction of being the only company to have adapted all of Sir Arthur Conan Doyle's Sherlock Holmes stories into audio dramas.[56]

A milestone in the medium occurred in the late 1970s, when film producer George Lucas sold the audio-drama adaptation rights for his *Star Wars* movie trilogy to his alma mater's radio station, KUSC FM, for three dollars.[57] The NPR affiliate then spent over $200,000 developing a thirteen-episode *Star Wars* audio-drama series that incorporated the talents of many of the movie's cast and crew.[58] Serialized audio-drama versions of *The Empire Strikes Back* and *Return of the Jedi* soon followed.[59]

In the 1980s, network audio-drama programs faded from the airwaves as productions from independent companies emerged. In 1982, ZBS debuted their science-fiction serial *Ruby: The Galactic Gumshoe*.[60] Two years later, the Atlanta Radio Theatre Company came on the scene with its program *SouthernAire Workshop*. They also performed live shows at conventions including DragonCon.[61] Both companies, which are still in operation today, were aided by the emerging audio-cassette market that enabled them to sell their productions directly to consumers. This helped them to develop and sustain their audience throughout the decade.

The Bronze Age of audio drama began in the mid-1990s, with the release of the MP3 audio-file format; it was in this period that CD and internet distribution of programs eclipsed the audio-cassette market.[62, 63] Producers such as Charles Potter and Random House began to release western audio dramas for radio airplay and consumer sale. Colonial Radio Theatre on the Air, Midwest Radio Theatre Workshop, and LA Theatre Works produced a large volume of original, high-quality content during this time.[64] In 1996, Jim French Productions debuted the syndicated audio-drama program *Imagination Theatre*. It was heard on stations across the country and featured an array of series such as *Kincaid, the StrangeSeeker*, *The Further Adventures of Sherlock Holmes*, and later *The Hilary Caine Mysteries*.[65]

The early 2000s saw a steady increase in independent audio-drama production aided by the continued growth of the internet. The Icebox Radio Theater began live and streamed performances of its original audio-drama series *The Scoop Sisters* and *The Crisper*. John Bells's family comedy show *Bell's in the Batfry* premiered in 2005 and quickly found a strong online following.[66] That same year audio dramatist, producer, and head of Sonic Cinema Productions (née Electric Vicuña Productions), Jack Ward, started *The Sonic Society*, a weekly series showcasing English-language audio dramas from the United States and Canada. The program was initially broadcast live on Canada's CKDU, but it soon transitioned to internet distribution and amassed fans from all corners of the globe.[67]

In 2009, Jack Ward and John Bell constructed a rating system for audio-drama programs. Ward followed this with several innovations, including producing the series *Sonic Speaks*, which featured interviews with audio-drama creators, and *Sonic Echo*, which showcased the best old-time radio shows.

His other initiatives included NADSWRIM—National Audio Drama Script Writers Month—a peer-incentivized writing program that encouraged audio dramatists to create new content.[68]

The Platinum Age of audio drama began in 2012 with the premiere of *Welcome to Night Vale.*[69] This series blended the genres of science fiction and comedy-drama into a satirical news broadcast that represented an innovative way of telling stories in the medium. By this point advancements in technology had brought about a major shift in the industry. Downloads and podcast series were the norm. Large companies, including Audible, Wondery, and Gimlet, took note and began producing content. Among the leaders of the era was New York–based producer Naomi Shah, who partnered with investors to amass over three million dollars in funding. This enabled her to produce *Meet Cute*, a fifteen-minute romantic comedy anthology series inspired by the work of writer/filmmaker Nora Ephron. Each episode featured a happily-ever-after feel, and was distributed through major audio-drama outlets.[70]

In 2018, Laurence Fishburne and Larenz Tate produced the African American audio-drama series *Bronzeville*. The program, based upon actual events, illuminated the history of how a lottery game helped sustain an African American community on the south side of Chicago during the 1940s. The show's rich storytelling, coupled with its Academy Award–winning cast and crew, helped draw new attention to the medium. In 2019, Aural Vision, LLC, acquired the catalog of Jim French Productions and assumed production of their popular series and the radio program *Imagination Theatre*, ensuring their continued success.[71] That same year, Jack Ward created the Mutual Audio Network, an on-demand streaming service that provided free audio-drama programming to listeners.[72] In 2021, Dramafy followed suit with a robust service of its own.

The long history of audio drama demonstrates its continued relevance as a storytelling medium. It was a major source of entertainment in its heyday and pioneered innovations such as syndication and the concept of the dramatic series. It empowered listeners and pushed the envelope of storytelling through programs such as *Lights Out* and *The Mercury Theatre on the Air*. Even during the downturn in its popularity, audio drama continued to forge new ground by telling gritty stories and incorporating natural noises into the sound effects that were used. CDs and the internet created a whole new listenership. The streaming and podcast technologies that are popular today have continued to increase access to the medium. Innovation, engaging storytelling, and modern subject matter will drive the industry forward. Keep these qualities in mind as you develop new audio dramas. They are key to success in the field now and in the future.

My Journey as an Audio Dramatist and What You Can Gain from It

Every summer when I was a teenager, I visited my aunt in Liverpool, New York, for a week. She loved stories of all kinds and had an audio-cassette collection of old-time radio shows. We listened to classics, including *The Abbott and Costello Show*, *Tarzan of the Apes*, and *The Lone Ranger*. I found the medium exciting because the audience got to create the visual component of the story in their mind. By the time I returned home after my first summer visit, I was hooked. I perused an old-time radio catalog my aunt gave me and started my own collection, ordering episodes from several series, my favorite being *My Favorite Husband*, which starred Lucille Ball. I listened to those shows over and over again.

Several years later, when I began my career as a playwright, I focused on writing one-act stage plays. All of my scripts received productions except for one. I shopped that play around to theaters for over a year, but none were interested. At that point, I thought back on my love for old-time radio and

decided to adapt the play into an audio drama. The script featured four characters, took place in two locations, and was dialogue driven. These qualities
made it easy to convert. Once the adaptation had been completed, I submitted it to an audio-drama production company. Two months later, they offered
me a contract and produced it. Little did I know that my career as an audio
dramatist had begun. Not long after that, I wrote another one-act stage play
that I was unable to get produced. I adapted it for audio and submitted it to
the same company I had earlier. They offered to produce it as well.

With two productions in the medium under my belt, I decided to join
an online community of audio dramatists. I came across an ad on their site
from a radio station that was looking to hire writers for a new audio-drama
anthology series. I applied and was offered a two-episode contract. The initial
scripts I wrote led to steady work. Shortly after, I became one of three staff
writers for the series. During that time, I adapted more of my one-act stage
plays into audio dramas and had them produced by a variety of companies.
A cold-call query letter led me to become a staff writer for one of the top-tier
audio-drama companies in the United States. I eventually went on to script
English-language audio dramas for a company in China and wrote a multi-
season western series for a radio station as well. Today I have more than fifty
audio-drama production credits and counting.

I included my journey as an audio dramatist here to illustrate that if you
want to work in the medium, it is within your reach. All you need is a desire
to write and determination. Despite what you may have heard, cold calls do
work—my journey is proof of that—but building professional relationships
over time is important as well, because it enables you to collaborate and grow
as a writer.

The chapters that follow guide you through the script development, submission, and production processes. Each contains insights that you can use to
become a working audio dramatist.

Chapter 2
Story Basics

Stories have existed for as long as human beings have. We tell them to each other every day. When you ask someone, "What happened?" you are asking that person to tell you a story. It's an integral part of life. Each of us is attracted to stories in literature and entertainment that speak to an aspect of life to which we can relate. It might be something we love, something we are having trouble dealing with, something we fear, or something we need to learn. Meaning is always at the core of a story, whether we realize it or not. The more broad or universal a story's meaning is, the more people it will resonate with.

Early in human history, stories were told orally. When physical recording methods such as writing were invented, many cultures started to document their stories in that way. Others continued to preserve and distribute their stories through the oral method. While physical recording cemented the exact word choice of a story and anchored it in a specific time period, the oral system allowed language and story details to evolve. Both oral and written forms offered different approaches to capture a story's core meaning.

Four thousand years ago, in the ancient region of Mesopotamia, the first notable piece of literature, *The Epic of Gilgamesh*, was written. Mythologists like Joseph Campbell would later cite it as a key example of the "hero's journey," a narrative form in which a main character (also known as the protagonist) embarks on a quest in pursuit of a goal, battling obstacles along the way. In the end, they are changed by the experience. In its broad outlines, the hero's journey can be found in stories of all kinds throughout history.

Storytelling Forms

Structured storytelling comes in many forms. Each has different characteristics, yet they all serve a similar function. Let's take a look at the most prominent types and discuss their value and purpose.

Song is a familiar form of storytelling. Its melody and rhythm engage us while its lyrics can describe ideas that convey a universal meaning about life. From spirituals that assure us something better is ahead to folk songs that capture life lessons in order to enlighten future generations, song is a popular and powerful method of storytelling on its own or when combined with other forms.

Fiction and nonfiction works, such as narrative poems, short stories, novellas, and novels, have the capacity to tell complex, nuanced stories. They can delve into a character's background and explore their inner thoughts and emotions. The audience engages with this type of story in an individual and personal way. When a story is in printed form, readers have the ability to revisit passages, allowing them to reflect on what's happened before they turn to the next page.

Stories for stage, screen, television, and audio drama unfold immediately in the audience's presence. Action and forward movement of plot are key. Characters' thoughts and inner experiences must manifest themselves in an active, external manner in order to be depicted. The dramatic form allows the audience to experience intimate storytelling that elicits emotion in a compact amount of time.

Essential Terms

The terms that follow are frequently used in dramatic storytelling. Most appear throughout this book. Their definitions are included here for clarity.

Antagonist. The character or force that stands in the way of the main character achieving their goal.

Drama. A scripted story that is performed for an audience. It features a character who is in conflict with themselves or others.

Genre. A category of story defined by unique, consistent qualities. For example, dramas depict story in a serious manner; comedies lace humor throughout their main character's journey; romance focuses on two individuals meeting and becoming enamored with one another; and westerns deal with the culture and mindset of characters living in the United States' Old West.

Plot. The ordering of events in a story to achieve a specific dramatic effect. A story may unfold in a linear way to show the incremental progression in a character's journey or in a nonlinear way, where select events are shown in a particular order to illustrate the story's point.

Protagonist. The main character in a story. The audience engages with the story in order to watch the protagonist's journey unfold.

Story. A set of circumstances, characters, and events written about to convey a given meaning.

Story Types

Over the years, various scholars and writers, including Joseph Campbell, William Foster-Harris, and Christopher Booker, have come up with different systems for categorizing stories. While there is no one "official" system, most of them identify the core components of a story similar to the following:

Man vs. man. The main character battles another character. Most stories fall into this category. Edgar Allan Poe's short story "The Cask of Amontillado" is an example. In it, a downtrodden man, Montresor, seeks to free himself from his so-called friend, Fortunato, who has continually prevented him from advancing in life.

Man vs. himself. The main character faces an internal struggle. One example is Chuck Palahniuk's novel *Fight Club*. It features a nameless protagonist who battles to overcome his tormented emotional state.

Man vs. nature. The main character fights a natural force. This type of story often centers on the challenge of surviving when separated from society. In Jack London's short story "To Build a Fire," for example, an unnamed miner falls through some ice in the wilderness and struggles to build a fire in an effort to dry off and stay alive.

Man vs. society. The main character combats an intangible, social obstacle. S.E. Hinton's novel *The Outsiders* is an example: a teenager battles a class system that stands in the way of him defining himself as an individual.

Man vs. technology. The main character encounters an outside force that is rooted in technology, as in Arthur C. Clarke's novel *2001: A Space Odyssey*. In that story, an astronaut, Dr. Dave Bowman, fights his ship's computer system in order to survive.

Story Communication Tools

A writer uses specific tools to tell a story. The medium they work in dictates which tools are available. Novelists, short story writers, and poets use all five of the senses to bring a story to life by describing sights, sounds, tastes, smells, and tactile aspects. Film and TV writers use two of the senses, sight and sound; visuals are their main tool, while sound is secondary. Playwrights use sight and sound as well, though sounds, such as dialogue, are the primary way of communicating story, while visuals are secondary.

Audio dramatists solely use sound to convey story. It is used in a variety of ways. Characters speak to express conflict and move the plot forward. Sound effects establish the story world and clarify dramatic moments. Music sets an underlying mood and may also be used to heighten dramatic tension. Audio-drama productions work hand in hand with their audience to bring a story to life. The medium's singular use of sound enables the listener to create the visual components of the story, including the characters and settings, in their mind. This quality makes audio drama one of the most intimate forms of dramatic storytelling.

Audio Drama, the "Poor Man's Screenwriting"

In some ways, audio drama can be seen as the "poor man's screenwriting." The reason for this is that everything done in a large-budget film can be accomplished in audio for a fraction of the cost. All production work for an audio-drama piece can be conducted in a physical or virtual studio with a few actors and microphones. The postproduction phase is usually completed in a matter of weeks, while in film it may take months. There are many free or inexpensive avenues available to distribute audio drama, including uploading productions onto syndication websites, selling digital downloads and CDs in the marketplace, and broadcasting on the air. All of this makes large-scale productions feasible in audio.

Story Length

The short form is the most popular length to tell a story in audio drama. It is categorized as a production that runs less than sixty minutes. Many companies produce content in the short form. Thirty-minute, stand-alone programs or serials are the most common. Series typically range anywhere from six to twelve episodes a season. Long-form or full-length productions have a running time of more than sixty minutes. Some companies produce audio dramas in this form. Adaptations of novels as well as original stories are a mainstay in this category. Regardless of how long a story is, you will find an audio-drama company that produces that length.

Chapter 3
Characters

Character is a core component of story. It brings the narrative to life and infuses it with meaning and emotion. How do you create a well-defined character? Let's start with a definition: A *character* is a unique being with specific traits, behaviors, and ways of thinking that set them apart from the rest of the individuals in their world. A character needs to have some degree of pathos or inner struggle in order to resonate with the audience.

Base Qualities of a Character

The elements that follow are core building blocks you can use to craft a character. As you read through them, bear in mind that each character you create needs to have both strengths and weaknesses. A story's protagonist is generally thought of in a positive manner, yet it is important they have shortcomings as well. Similarly, an antagonist may be seen as a negative force within the story, but they should have some redeeming qualities. Characters that are a blend of contrasting attributes will have depth and a realness to them that resonates with the listener. With this said, let's look at the key components required to construct a character.

Physical appearance. How does a character look? The style of clothes, height, weight, and other features define a character's physical presence, which may affect how others view and interact with them. A good-looking character might be treated more kindly than someone with average features. Likewise, someone with a large physical presence may have people step out of their way, while an individual who is slight in build might be pushed aside.

Likes and dislikes. What does a character enjoy, and what turns them off? The qualities in life that give someone pleasure or that they disdain provide insight into who they are. A character who likes order might find it difficult to deal with someone who has no sense of organization. Likewise, an individual who enjoys peace and quiet may find it challenging to live next door to a rock band.

Fears and phobias. What scares a character, and how does that fear affect them? Things that cause apprehension in a character speak to their limitations. An individual who has an anxiety about insects might be reluctant to go into a dark, dirty area, while someone who frets about what others think of them might shy away from people.

Strengths. What are a character's talents and positive attributes? The skills that an individual possesses may affect how others perceive them and how they perceive themselves. A character who is a good cook might be able to use that skill to attract friends, while someone who is adept with logic may excel at solving problems.

Weaknesses. What does a character find to be a challenge? This will shape what they do and what others think about them. If a character is extremely talkative, it could be a mask for their inadequacies. If a character is not skilled at sports but likes to participate in them, their self-esteem may be affected if they are not picked for a team when playing with friends.

What a character reveals about themself. What parts of oneself does an individual let others see? The attributes a character shares about themself may affect the way others view them. If someone uses humor to get through challenges in life, it shows that they have resilience. On the other hand, if someone takes pleasure in running animals down on the highway, it illustrates their callous nature toward other living creatures.

What a character hides about themself. What aspects of a character's life don't they talk about and why? Knowing what a character hides and what is at stake for them if that information is exposed gives insight into the character. If an individual was convicted of embezzlement, they may conceal it when applying for a job as a cashier. Likewise, someone who is self-conscious about a disease they have may not disclose it out of fear that it may drive others away from them.

A character's upbringing. How did childhood experiences affect a character? Fleshing out the early years of an individual's life will give insight into the choices they make during the story. If someone bounced from foster home to foster home during their formative years, they may find it challenging to attach emotionally to others, while someone who was given false praise as a child may believe they are more talented than they actually are.

Whom a character associates with. What kind of individuals comprise a character's inner circle? The people someone brings into their world are telling of the qualities they value in others. If the bulk of someone's friends are dock workers, they may relate most strongly to a blue-collar viewpoint. On the other hand, if a character has a diverse group of friends, they may have insight into people from varied backgrounds.

Socioeconomic background. How does a character's social and financial level in society affect their prospects in life? The amount of affluence someone has impacts their views and their potential. An individual who doesn't have much education or opportunity may not be able to advance beyond the limited scope of their world, while someone whose life is filled with prosperity may see opportunity everywhere.

Where a character lives. Do they live in an apartment, a house, or a mobile home? Are they located in a city, the suburbs, or the country? The environment in which someone lives may shape their views and the way they behave. A character who lives in a crowded city and encounters people daily might be well-adjusted socially, while someone who lives alone in the backwoods may find socializing to be a challenge.

Time period. How does the era in which a story takes place affect a character's behavior? The rules and social norms of the period in which a character lives shape their understanding of how the world works and what is possible for them within it. If a free-spirited individual lives during an age when most things are forbidden, they might be forced to suppress their spontaneity so they are not shunned by society. Conversely, if a free-spirited character lives during an era when anything goes, they would feel free to express themselves openly and might even be seen as typical.

Religion. Does a character practice a specific religion? If so, are they a staunch believer, or do they struggle with their faith? An individual's perspective on religion can influence their outlook on life, including how they view and treat others and themselves. Someone with unwavering spiritual beliefs may have set principles to guide them, while someone who does not have a faith may need to determine how they will value and navigate life.

Social position. Has society treated a character with fairness, cast them
aside, or put undue burdens on them solely because of their social
status? A character's relationship with their community and where
they fit within it shapes how they see themselves, others, and the
world. If a marginalized individual runs for political office, they may
not be taken seriously because of their limited means. On the other
hand, someone with greater social status might enjoy more notoriety
and power.

Self-worth. Does a character value who they are, value others more than
themselves, or abuse themselves? The degree of respect a character
shows to themselves says a lot about their self-esteem and inner life.
An individual who inflicts pain on their body in the hope that others
will show concern is struggling to value themselves, while a character
who believes in themselves should have the confidence needed to
succeed in their endeavors.

What a character thinks about others. Do they see the people they interact with as equal, superior, or less than themselves? The value a character ascribes to others says a lot about how they see themselves and
the world. If someone considers those they encounter as predators,
they may find life to be treacherous, while an individual who believes
others are not as important as they are may discover that they have
little when it comes to heartfelt connections with others.

Life-shaping events. What are the milestones in a character's life? Experiences affect an individual and may change their outlook. Someone
who has had everything given to them expects things to go their way,
while someone who was used by others when they needed them the
most may be reluctant to trust anyone.

What a character thinks about the world. How does an individual view
life and their place within it? A character's perspective on their own

existence determines their mindset about their fate. If someone sees the world as bigger than they are, they may feel they are powerless to change things. On the other hand, if a character views life's limitations as an asset, they may be able to use them to advance themself in the world.

How a character handles relationships. In what ways does a character navigate friendships and alliances? The manner in which someone manages the complexities of a relationship reveals the strength of their social skills. One individual may turn a blind eye on issues until they fester into an irreparable mess, while another may keep communication open and work through problems as they arise so they can have more fulfilling relationships overall.

Problem-solving ability. Is a character resourceful, indecisive, or prone to casting their problems off on others? The way a character deals with challenges says a lot about who they are and their ability to succeed. A character who cannot make up their mind may be destined to fail, while someone who makes impulsive decisions may have an uneven track record when it comes to success.

Backstory

As a writer, it is important to know what happened to a character before they first appear in a script. These details are known as backstory. You can never know too much about the characters you create. Once you have developed their core attributes, take time to explore their background. Consider the following basic aspects when you do.

What led a character to be in the story? Define the circumstances that led a character to be part of the situation that is depicted in the script. Was it something they intended to do? Was it a surprise? Were they forced into it? Do they stand to gain anything from being in the situation? Do they regret their involvement? How do the other participants feel about the situation and each other being involved in it? Having insight into how the main situation in the story came about will make it easier for you to write the script because you'll understand the reason why it occurred.

<u>What led a character to be in the location where the story takes place?</u> Determine how well a character knows the area in which the story is set. Do they live there? Did they grow up there? Are they just passing through? Do they like or dislike the location? If so, why? Whom do they know in town, and how well do they know them? Have they had experiences that shaped their perspective of the area? If so, what are they? Understanding a character's relationship to the story's location will give you insight into how familiar they are with the people, places, and events that occurred there and why the character behaves as they do in the story.

<u>Why is a character friends with another character?</u> Define the relationship between a character and other individuals in the story so you understand when they met and what led them to become friends. On what do they see eye to eye? On what do they have opposing views? What was the most impactful moment in their relationship? What was the best time they shared together? What secrets do they keep from each other? Having insight into these aspects will enable you to craft a dynamic relationship between the characters.

<u>Why does one character not like another character?</u> Understanding what led one character to be in conflict with another is an essential part of developing a story. Where did the characters meet? What led to their discord? Does one character like the other, but the other doesn't like them? Is there anything upon which they agree? Is the conflict

between them reparable? How do their family and friends feel about the tension between them? Exploring the origins of their relationship and their conflict will allow you to have a full understanding of how each character will act toward the other during the story.

How does the dynamic between the main character and the supporting characters shape the story? Identify significant backstory moments between the main character and each of the supporting characters that defines the trajectory of their relationship going forward. What brought about these events? How did they affect the characters' relationship? Understanding the dynamics between the main character and the other characters will help you to see why the characters took certain actions that shaped the story.

Ways to Communicate Character in Audio Drama

Once you have established the core elements and the backstory for each character, the next step is to determine how these aspects will be communicated in the script. There are several methods you can use to do that, which include the following:

Action and behavior. Think about how a character's personality, fears, likes, and dislikes affect the way they behave in the story. Do they shy away from conflict or act aggressively? Base how a character responds to the situations in the story on how their life experiences have shaped them up until that point.

Word choice. The words a character says give insight into who they are. Do they use slang? Swear? Throw big words around to elevate their social position in life? Does the character use phrases such as "in my day" or "ya know"? Word choice gives the audience insight into where a character came from, their education level, and what their temperament is.

Thought process. The way a character understands the world and where they fit within it dictates the kind of decisions they make in a story. Are a character's thoughts scattered? Do they discount their own judgment in lieu of others' advice? Consider how their fears, secrets, and strengths affect the choices they make. These will help you understand how they will react in any situation.

What other characters say. What other characters say about a character when they are not around can give insight into the character. Is the character referred to in a respectful way? Are their faults the focus of the conversation? Is caution used when discussing the character? Other characters' perspective can give dimension to a character by revealing aspects that have not been expressed before.

Diverse situations. How a character behaves in various settings provides insight into who they are. Do they act one way during a crisis, another in a courtroom, and yet another when they are with a close friend? Putting a character in diverse situations brings out their strengths, weaknesses, and idiosyncrasies which will give them dimension.

Putting Theory into Practice—A Case Study on Character Development

Let's put the concepts discussed in this chapter into practice by looking at an example of how to construct a character. We'll start with a basic situation:

College student and jewelry store clerk Jack Brayden is pulled over one night by the police. Several containers of missing silver and gold rings are found in his trunk. He is charged with theft and must prove his innocence or risk losing the respect of his community, his academic scholarship, and most importantly, his freedom.

Now that we know some key facts, the next step is to flesh out who the protagonist is.

Jack Brayden

Base Qualities

Physical appearance. Jack is twenty years old, five-foot-eight, with a fit body, and weighs 159 pounds. He prefers to wear jeans and T-shirts but dresses in khakis and a button-down shirt on the job because it is required. Jack is considered above average looking and receives a little extra attention from people because of it.

Likes and dislikes. He doesn't snack much but likes a juicy hamburger with everything on it and a beer from time to time. He isn't old enough to drink, so friends get it for him. Jack enjoys listening to heavy metal music. He can't stand ballet and other so-called arts. He has a mildly crude sense of humor and expresses it with his friends. He likes busting out on the back roads and driving recklessly when he can.

Fears and phobias. Jack worries about being confined in small spaces because it makes him feel trapped. He has had a fear of being locked up ever since he was eight years old, when his father was arrested. Jack hasn't heard from his father since.

Strengths. Math was his strongest subject in high school. Jack's mathematical aptitude helped him get a college scholarship, while his personality enabled him to get hired at the jewelry store after he moved to Mansfield, Pennsylvania. He is well-liked by most of his coworkers and goes the extra mile to help his customers. Jack is a good listener and generous with friends and family.

<u>Weaknesses.</u> Sports are not Jack's strong suit, but he likes to watch them, especially football and hockey. He has poor spelling and grammar skills. Jack's eyesight is bad, although he corrects it by wearing contacts. He enjoys cooking but isn't very good at it and frequently burns what he makes. Jack is not skilled when it comes to managing money. He tends to splurge on fun things only to discover he doesn't have enough left to pay important bills.

<u>What a character reveals about themself.</u> Jack is rather private and only tells his troubles to close friends. He focuses on the positive aspects of his life when talking with his coworkers.

<u>What a character hides about themself.</u> He tends not to express his opinion if it differs from those he's with because he fears they will reject him. He doesn't discuss what happened to his father with friends or coworkers because he worries they will shun him if they knew the truth.

<u>A character's upbringing.</u> Jack was close with his father until his father was sent to prison. After that, he was raised by his mother. She did her best to get by, but it was a struggle at times. Jack's mother remarried when he was a freshman in high school. There was some friction between him and his stepfather. He saw Jack as an obstacle in his relationship with Jack's mother. This left Jack feeling like an outsider in his own family at times.

<u>Whom a character associates with.</u> Jack has an eclectic circle of friends. In high school, he rode with a dirt-bike group. He continued his friendship with two of his dirt-bike buddies after he stopped riding. They are Ana (rugged, not afraid of a few bruises from riding) and Stew (a competitive daredevil who hates to lose). Jack and Stew even went to the same college and worked at the jewelry store together. Jack maintained a friendship with him until Stew became annoyed that Jack

got a raise instead of him. Stew hasn't returned Jack's calls or messages since. Jack also maintained a friendship with Mr. Wolawski, a P.E. teacher at his high school who ran the archery club. Mr. Wolawski is friends with the jewelry store owners and has seen Jack there a few times when he has come in to chat with them. Karen-Anne, or K.A., as she is called by her friends, is Jack's former girlfriend. They dated for three years and had a bad breakup one year before the story starts. She became tired of Jack not spending enough time with her, so she started dating his friend, Milt, behind his back. Jack was devastated that they betrayed him in such a way. He hasn't spoken to either of them since. Now that Jack is in college, he has some drinking buddies. Most are college sophomores who get alcohol through upperclassmen and share it with Jack. When he drinks, he slurs his words and tends to use crude humor.

Socioeconomic background. When Jack was eight, his parents rented a house in a middle-class neighborhood. He had a small set of friends there with whom he was close. That same year, Jack's father was convicted of numerous counts of bank fraud and went to prison. After he was locked up, Jack's mother could no longer afford the house. She divorced her husband and rented a low-income apartment a few towns away. Jack had to make new friends there. Money was tight. Jack's mother worked as a receptionist at a small company in town until her job was phased out. After that, she did temp work, moving from one short-term assignment to another for the next six years. During that time, she struggled to afford the essentials in life. That changed when she started dating the manager at one of her temp jobs. She eventually married him. Jack and his mother moved into his stepfather's house so they could have an easier life as a dual-income family. Jack had to leave his friends yet again when they moved. He spent the second half of his freshman year all the way through his senior year in a new high school. The family lived in an affluent area, although they didn't have as much as most families there did. Jack tended to hang out with people at school whose families were in a similar financial situation to his.

Where a character lives. The story opens with Jack in his second year of college in Mansfield, Pennsylvania, a borough of about 2,900 people. He moved there a year and a half ago to go to school on an academic scholarship. He is majoring in mathematics. Pay disparities in town are large, with men making $10,000 more a year than women. Mansfield has a close-knit feel. People are friendly and help one another. Jack is comfortable there, although there are social expectations he is just starting to understand. The more he learns about them, the less he likes it there.

Time period. The story is set in the present day. Technology is quickly replacing face-to-face communication more and more in Jack's world. Education and professional status determine a person's financial and social worth within the community. Stress is low. Life expectancy is equal to the national average.

Religion. Jack's mother was raised as an Episcopalian. She wasn't very religious as an adult but had Jack baptized and confirmed into the church. They stopped attending services after that because she had to work more to make ends meet. On a day-to-day basis, Jack doesn't reflect much on religion. He believes in the concepts of heaven and hell and right and wrong and feels everyone should treat one another fairly.

Social position. At this point in life, Jack sees himself as an average citizen who is living his life. He thinks it's wrong that men get paid more for doing the same job that his mother does. He respects the law but doesn't like being talked down to by anyone.

Self-worth. He takes pride in his appearance and sees himself as a normal, likeable guy. He wants a career that will make him happy. In the moment, that consists of working as a clerk at the jewelry store. He isn't sure what the future holds.

What a character thinks about others. Jack tries to treat people with respect. He loves his mother dearly. He feels his stepfather is manipulative at times, but he does his best to get along with him since he makes his mother happy. He perceives his boss as firm and very exacting about how employees should comport themselves at work. He hasn't had a lot of experience with diversity but likes to think he treats everyone equally, unless they annoy him.

Life-shaping events. Jack was disappointed in his father for abandoning him when he went to prison. It left a hole in his life. He longed for his mother to attend his school events, but she was never able to get off of work. He blames his father for this: if he hadn't committed those crimes, his mother would have been able to be there to support him. The discord between Jack and his stepfather drove Jack to do well in high school so he could get into college and move out on his own as soon as he graduated.

What a character thinks about the world. He sees life as a path he has to go on like everyone else. He doesn't want to be the best. He just wants to get by and find some degree of happiness along the way. He isn't concerned about death because he thinks of it as for the old or terminally ill. He feels he missed a lot of family connections because his father's parents severed ties with him and his mother after their son went to prison—they believe Jack's mother constantly badgered their son to get her expensive things, driving him to commit crimes. They refuse to have anything to do with her or Jack because of this. This led Jack to feel the world can be very unfair at times.

How a character handles relationships. If Jack is not treated well, he tends to keep his feelings pent up. After he and K.A. broke up, he refused to acknowledge the pain he felt over their separation, even though it still simmers within him. Jack feels conflicted about the relationship he has with his stepfather because his stepfather spends most of his time with Jack's mother.

Problem-solving ability. Solving problems is not his strong suit, but nonetheless he tries to tackle them. It takes him a long time to forget things, which can create anxiety when new issues arise. When they do, he is his own worst enemy because he puts himself through unnecessary stress.

Backstory

The next step in developing Jack's character is filling in missing details about his life. Important elements touched on in the section above can be fleshed out below if they provide insight into the character's role in the story.

What led a character to be in the story? Jack is in the story because he is suspected of stealing from his employer. Earlier in the school year, a police officer pulled Jack over for going through a yellow light. The officer claimed he was cutting it too close and should have stopped. He gave Jack a warning. In the story, the same police officer pulls Jack over for a burnt-out taillight. The police recently received a tip that jewelry was stolen from the store Jack works at. When the officer sees Jack's driver's license, he recognizes Jack's name from a list of employees supplied by the jewelry store. This prompts the officer to look in his trunk and find containers of jewelry. Jack is unable to explain how they got there and is arrested and ultimately charged with theft.

<u>What led a character to be in the location where the story takes place?</u>
Jack moved to Mansfield, Pennsylvania, to attend college. He is
familiar with the town and is just starting to learn about its history
and how society works there.

<u>Why is a character friends with another character?</u> Jack's high school P.E.
teacher, Mr. Wolawski, thinks Jack is a good kid and tries to support
him. After Jack is charged with theft, Mr. Wolawski is one of a few
people to whom Jack can turn. Jack was a good student in his class
and even helped Mr. Wolawski by getting signatures on a petition to
support him getting tenure. That meant a lot to Mr. Wolawski and
showed Jack's compassion for others. Mr. Wolawski saw Jack leave
school early on senior cut day but didn't say anything. He understood it was a onetime event. He never mentioned it to anyone,
although he and Jack made eye contact as Jack left that day. A year
after Jack graduated, they had lunch and caught up on each other's
lives. Jack knew he had a friend and mentor in Mr. Wolawski after
that. It meant a lot.

<u>Why does one character not like another character?</u> Jack's friend Stew
also works at the jewelry store. He thinks Jack is trying to kiss up to
the owners to get a raise. Stew has worked a lot of overtime and feels
he deserves the raise Jack received. Jack has noticed Stew's hostility
due to him getting the raise, including when Stew did not hold the
door for him. He keeps his feelings inside and plans to continue
being nice to Stew in the hope things will turn around in their relationship. Meanwhile, Stew's frustration with the situation and Jack
only grows.

<u>How does the dynamic between the main character and supporting char-
acters shape the story?</u> Jack's friendship with Stew deteriorates when
Stew's jealousy over Jack getting the raise instead of him intensifies.

It leads Stew to bad-mouth Jack to the police, saying that Jack was a delinquent in high school, frequently cut class, and stole money from people's coats during a dance. Stew's claims are printed in the newspaper. They hurt Jack's reputation. The prosecution plans to use the information against Jack if the case goes to trial. The reality is that Jack and Stew cut class together on senior cut day. Stew also convinced Jack to search through people's coats at the dance with him. Stew kept most of the money they found, which amounted to about fifty dollars. When Jack tries to tell the truth about the situation, no one will listen, which frustrates him and doesn't help the case against him.

Now that you have read the case study, reflect on it and note how the experiences a character has and the qualities they possess affect their behavior. They can also influence the story's plot. Bear these aspects in mind when you develop a character.

Helpful Hints: The Top Five Reasons Audiences Don't Connect with a Character and How to Avoid Them

1. A character behaves in ways that are not consistent with how they have been established at the beginning of the script.

    Verify that each action a character makes is consistent with their thought process and sensibilities. If an action isn't consistent with who they are, think up an action that is and incorporate it into the script.

2. A character talks but never acts.

    If this occurs, establish a challenge for the character to face and force them to combat it.

3. A character drives the story forward through their actions, but the audience never sees their emotional side.

   In this instance, give the character strengths and weaknesses that manifest themselves through the actions they take and reveal their inner struggle in the process.

4. A character is one-dimensional.

   Explore the character's interests, likes/dislikes, decision-making skills, fears/phobias, and other qualities that define them. Verify that these qualities are unique and encompass their joys and pains. Incorporate some of these elements into how the character behaves in the script. This will flesh out the character and give them dimension in the process.

5. A character is predictable.

   Create a list of the decisions the character makes in the script that feel expected. Brainstorm other choices they can make in that moment that will turn the story in an unexpected way and provide insight into who they are.

Character profiles are a valuable resource that can evolve as you develop a script. The information you discover while creating them will enrich the story you are telling and accelerate your writing process as well.

Chapter 4
Dialogue

Dialogue is an essential tool for the audio dramatist. On the surface, it may appear to simply be the words that a character speaks, but there is a lot more to those words than meets the eye. They communicate intent and emotion, and create conflict. They also help the audience to define what each character looks like in their mind. In this chapter, we will explore the use of dialogue and how to construct it.

One key function of dialogue is to provide insight into the characters. When someone encounters an obstacle, they are faced with making a decision. For example, if a person is trapped in a room, they might call for help, try to get the door open, panic, or sit calmly and wait for someone to come. The way a character reacts gives the audience understanding into the type of person they are. That information is expressed through dialogue.

Levels of Dialogue
The manner in which a character uses dialogue to communicate meaning is based upon their needs, the situation they are in, and whom they are talking

with. Each line a character says falls into one of the three levels of dialogue. Let's take a look at each.

Level 1: Say exactly what you mean. If a character needs to be direct, such as in a business transaction, they will use this level. For example, a patron at a car wash may say, "Give me a normal wash." A movie-goer could request, "Two tickets for the seven thirty show, please." A detective during an interrogation might ask, "Why did you do it?" These statements clearly communicate a base need from one character to another in a direct way.

Level 2: Refer indirectly to what you mean. When two characters are familiar with each other, they tend to communicate through shorthand. The type of shorthand they use is based upon the dynamics in their relationship. For example, a longtime assistant at a bakery may say to their coworker, "I've done enough cleaning. It's time you-know-who does it for a change," implying that another coworker needs to pitch in sometimes. Similarly, a parent might encourage their irresponsible child, "You'd better get busy if you know what's good for you," indicating that they will be punished if they do not act. One fishing buddy on a boat might say to another, "Sit down unless you want to take a swim again," alluding to an earlier mishap he fears could be repeated. Each of these exchanges communicates meaning the characters understand based upon their past experiences together.

Level 3: Say one thing but mean something else. When characters know each other well, they share a common knowledge and history. In this level of dialogue, meaning lies under the surface of the words that are said. For example, a wife may say to her husband, "It would be nice if I didn't have to wash these by hand," meaning, *When are you going to fix the dishwasher?* A football player might use sarcasm with their teammate and say, "You never slip up, do you?" meaning that their teammate talks a good game, but in reality makes a lot of errors. A grown son might tell his mother, "Any time you want to come over, you're welcome to," suggesting that his mother never comes to visit. The audience will understand the meaning of these lines because the dynamics between the characters and their situation have been established already.

Speech Pattern

Each of us has our own way of speaking, which is composed of our choice of words, the cadence of our speech, and the underlying meaning of what we say. The characters we create need to have their own unique voice as well. If you pick up a script, you should be able to read the dialogue without looking at the character names and know exactly who is speaking. "How do you craft dialogue with such distinct qualities?," you may ask. It starts with a bit of detective work.

"Grassroots" quote collection is an important technique to use in the dialogue creation process. To get started on this process, listen to people you know or overhear and jot down the words they say that contain unique grammar, speech patterns, or phrases that intrigue you.

When you develop a period piece, locate court transcripts, newspaper interviews, or first-person accounts from the era in which your story takes place. Write down dialogue that stands out to you. Bear in mind that the setting in which a person speaks might influence their word choice. Someone giving testimony in a courtroom might use different language than they would if they were chatting with a friend in their kitchen. Despite the limitations found in the sources of a given period, these documents are a valuable resource.

If you are working on a true story, compile a set of quotes people said in newspaper articles, letters, diaries, emails, and other media. If you have access to any of the individuals who were involved in the story, meet with them and record your discussion. Take note of their word choices and how they use the three levels of dialogue.

Once you have finished gathering quotes, consolidate them, keeping only those that will help you construct an authentic speech pattern for the characters in your script. After you have done so, you are ready for the next step, the creation of a character speech dictionary.

Character Speech Dictionary

A character speech dictionary houses the words that make up a character's speech pattern. After you have gathered quotes, set up a spreadsheet or a table and insert each character's name from a script you are developing at the top of a separate column. Once that has been completed, review the dialogue in your script and enter any unique phrases a character says in the column that corresponds with their name. Then, look over the spreadsheet and determine if two or more characters use the same phrase. If that occurs, consider assigning the phrase to one character, unless there is a story-driven reason for both of them to say it.

The next step is to review the quotes you gathered from conversations and other sources and use it to flesh out each character's speech pattern. Determine which words or phrases feel authentic to which characters and enter them in that character's column on the spreadsheet. It is not necessary for all characters to have the same number of phrases in the dictionary, but they should have enough to individualize their voice. Once this step has been completed, review the dictionary entries again. You should get a sense of who each character is by the entries that appear under their name. If there are characters who continue to have a low number of unique words to say, think about who they are and find words that are authentic to the way they talk.

Below is a sample character speech dictionary. It is based upon the character of Jack and his world that was discussed in chapter 3. Use it as a guide to create your own dictionary.

Jack	Mr. Wolawski	Jack's Stepfather	Jack's Mother
Aw, man!	Longbow (nickname for Jack)	Boy (to Jack)	Hey, scout (to Jack only)
I'm gonna bail (meaning leave)	Know you	You hear me	Hang in there
Uh-huh	You got this	Jeez	Dumb bunnies
You bet	Rough time	Have some guts	Payday (meaning celebration)
Come on	Don't know	She's beat (meaning tired)	You're so sweet
Beaut	Could be	Pass the buck	Don't cop out
You're tellin' me	Ease up	Rat hole	Be straight now
Whatever	Good to go	Slacker	Honey (to stepfather only)
That's epic	No biggie	Stand up	Cool down
Yes, sir/Yes, ma'am	No sweat	Use your gourd	Sharp

After your speech dictionary is populated, do a pass of your script looking at one character's dialogue at a time and revise it as needed to flesh out each character's unique voice. Make sure the dialogue sounds authentic. If a character speaks in slang, it might not sound natural for them to use it every time they say a particular word. Consider alternating the use of specific words. A character in an audio drama I wrote used the slang word "yuh'" instead of "you." To make their dialogue sound more authentic, I replaced several occurrences of "yuh" with "you" when the context merited it. This subtle change made the character's dialogue feel realistic.

More on Dialogue

A character's word choice is influenced by their life experiences, the cultural group of which they are a part, their profession, who they are as a person, and other aspects as well. Let's look at some phrases and how various characters might say them. The first column in the chart below features basic phrases. That is followed by character types and the words they may use to express each basic phrase.

Phrase	Nun	Teenager	Waitress	Surfer
I love you	You're a dear	Love ya	It's always a pleasure to serve you	I got you
Leave	I don't want to keep you	Go	Thank you for coming	Better split, dude
Pay me	Please, leave an offering	Where is it?	Here's your bill	Throw me some cash
Hello	Good day	Hi	Nice to see you	Ay
Goodbye	Take care, my child	Bye	Have a good day	Ciao

Phrase	Nun	Teenager	Waitress	Surfer
What time is it?	Would you be so kind as to tell me the time?	Got the time?	Do you know the time?	What's the hour, bro?
I'm tired	The Lord is calling me in for the night	I'm beat	I'm exhausted	I'm burnt, man
Thank you	Bless your heart	I owe you one	I appreciate it	You're the best
You're welcome	My pleasure	No problem	If there's anything else you need, let me know	Any time
May I help you?	What can I do for you, child?	Is there something I can do?	I'm happy to help if you need it	Need something?

Look at the characters in the story you're developing and consider how they would say the phrases in the chart above. Add each character's unique expression of the phrases to your story's character speech dictionary to further develop their voice.

Now that we have explored the tools and methods you can use to craft a character's individual voice, let's look at how they can be used in a script. The example that follows features the character of Jack and his situation.

(Jail cell ambiance)

SOUND: FILTERED - A PHONE RINGS.

                    JACK'S STEPFATHER
              (filtered, on phone)
Hello.

                    JACK
Is Mom there?

                    JACK'S STEPFATHER
              (filtered, on phone)
Jack? Is that you?

                    JACK
Yeah. Could you put her on?

                    JACK'S STEPFATHER
              (filtered, on phone)
Do you know what time it is?

                    JACK
Mom, please?

                    JACK'S STEPFATHER
              (filtered, on phone)
Where are you?

                    JACK
Don't worry about it.

                    JACK'S STEPFATHER
              (filtered, on phone)
Where are you?

                    JACK
Could you make things easy for once?

                    JACK'S STEPFATHER
              (filtered, on phone)
She's beat.

                    JACK
I have a right to talk to her, you know.

                              JACK'S STEPFATHER
                       (filtered, on phone)
          We all have rights.

                              JACK
          Come on.

                              JACK'S STEPFATHER
                       (filtered, on phone)
          Stop passin' the buck and get home.

                              JACK
          That's why I'm calling.

                              JACK'S STEPFATHER
                       (filtered, on phone)
          If it is, then don't be a slacker.

                              JACK
          Please, put her on.

              SOUND: A BEEP.

                              JACK'S STEPFATHER
                       (filtered, on phone)
          What was that?

                              JACK
          I don't have time to go into it. Put her on.

                              JACK'S STEPFATHER
                       (filtered, on phone)
          You really think you're somethin' special,
          don'tcha?

                              JACK
          Please. I have to go soon.

                              JACK'S STEPFATHER
                       (filtered, on phone)
          Then out with it already.

                              JACK
                       (reluctant)
          I'm-- in jail.

>   JACK'S STEPFATHER
>   (filtered, on phone)
> What?

>   JACK
> They accused me of stealing, but I didn't do
> it. Will you let me talk to her?

>   JACK'S STEPFATHER
>   (filtered, on phone)
> Jeez, what the hell are they teachin' you at
> that school, boy?

>   JACK
> Thanks for understanding.

>   JACK'S STEPFATHER
>   (filtered, on phone)
> You need to grow up.

>   JACK
> I need a lawyer. Will you put her on, please?
> I am her son, you know.

>   SOUND: A CLICK.

>   JACK (cont'd)
> Hello? . . . Hello? . . .

>   SOUND: JACK SIGHS IN FRUSTRATION.

>   JACK
> Aw, man!

Take note of how word choice and the different levels of dialogue come into play in the scene above. The language that each character uses establishes their speech pattern, demonstrates the relationship between them, and gives insight into how they look. The history the characters share adds a tension that lies under the surface. It is expressed in several ways, including the use of third-level dialogue, which can be seen when Jack says, "I am her son," meaning "I am more important to her than you are." Dialogue can also enhance the audience's ability to visualize a character, such as when Jack's stepfather says, "Jeez, what the hell are they teachin' you at that school, boy?" This line projects a gruffness that enables listeners to create how the character looks in their mind. All of these aspects are communicated solely through the use of dialogue and help define the characters.

Helpful Hints: Five Ways to Create Vibrant Character Dialogue

1. Avoid having characters use clichéd language.
2. Pepper in original phrases that are specific to a given character.
3. Incorporate regionalisms and slang into a character's dialogue.
4. Give a character a unique cadence to their speech. Examples include frequent use of one-word responses, speaking in short phrases, or using complex sentences.
5. Express a character's personality in the words they choose to say.

Crafting dialogue is a skill that takes time to master. The more you work at it, the more adept you will become. Review the techniques discussed in this chapter again as needed and then implement them. Doing so will enhance your skills as a writer and make the scripts you develop all the better for it when they are done.

Chapter 5
Scenes

A scene is one of the main building blocks of a dramatic script. It is defined as an event that occurs in a specific location at a specific time. Whenever there is a change of place, a new scene begins. Any time there is a gap in time, that requires the start of a new scene as well. If two bandits have a shootout in a bar and a sheriff chases them outside, the moment that they move outside, a new scene begins. Similarly, if a sheriff interrogates a witness in a bar, then five minutes later the sheriff discusses the incident with a colleague in the same bar, the gap in time between those two events creates two separate scenes.

Each scene is like a miniature story. It has a beginning, a middle, and an end. It needs to include characters, dramatic tension, and advance the plot. If a scene doesn't move the story forward, it should provide insight into the characters. If none of these elements are present, they need to be added or the scene will be ineffective and should be removed from the script. Begin each scene as close to the dramatic point you intend to make with that moment in the story and end right after the point has been made. This will keep the audience's interest level strong and leave them wanting to know what happens next.

In an audio-drama script, scenes are numbered and labeled. Numbers provide distinct reference points, while labels identify the location and the underlying ambient sounds that are inherent to them. For example:

<pre>
                    Scene 9
            (Jail cell ambiance)
</pre>

This lets everyone involved in the production know at what point in the script the scene occurs and what location it occurs in. The numbering of scenes also enables production staff to easily reference specific sections of a script when scheduling material for rehearsal and recording. Scene numbers and labels have value during the postproduction process as well. Numbers enable the editor to identify a scene so it can be placed properly in the story's timeline. This is especially important when scenes are recorded out of order. Scene labels clarify location, which is useful during recording sessions and in postproduction when it comes to the selection of ambient sounds to include in a scene.

It is important to establish a sense of place at the start of every scene. Since listeners are not able to see a location, the setting needs to be clarified quickly through the use of soundscape, dialogue, or a combination of the two. If a scene takes place on the beach, it could open with an underlying soundscape of waves rolling up on the shore, a lifeguard's whistle blowing, or footsteps walking on wet sand. If sounds don't immediately make the location apparent, characters can use dialogue to help clarify the setting. There are two ways to do this. Option #1: A mother could say, "Doesn't the water look beautiful today?" Option #2: The mother could say, "I don't see Danny out there. Isn't that his life vest? I told him not to go in without it." The first option clarifies location. The second option establishes a sense of place and creates tension. If the next scene occurs in a similar place, such as a boat in the ocean, it is important to set up the location, so the audience understands they are no longer on the beach. This can be accomplished by starting the scene with a boat rocking in the ocean, having someone paddle oars through the waves, or having an engine buzz as it propels a boat through rough water. Initial dialogue could have the boat captain saying, "I see something red down there. What color bathing suit was Danny wearing?" Since both scenes occur at the shore, it is important to include sounds that represent the specific location at the top of each scene, along with clarifying dialogue. By including these qualities, the listener will have an immediate sense of where each scene occurs.

The number of characters you include in a scene can affect the audience's comprehension of the story. The more characters there are, the more challenging it may be for the listener to keep track of them. If it is essential that a large number of characters be in a specific scene, establish each of them clearly when they first enter and then have them talk occasionally throughout the scene. For example, if a group of friends was on a museum tour, their presence could be established at the start of the scene by the tour guide or by the friends themselves. After that, each character could speak a few times. If you use this approach, it will keep all of the characters in the forefront of the audience's mind as the scene progresses.

The Scene: A Practical Example

Now that we have discussed the qualities that make up a scene, let's look at how those qualities play out in scripted form. The following example is based upon the character Jack and his situation.

Scene 15
(Grocery store ambiance)

SOUND: A SLIDING DOOR SHUTS.

SOUND: FOOTSTEPS.

SOUND: SHOPPING-CART METAL CLINKS
TOGETHER.

                    STEW
Hands off. This shopping cart is mine.

                    JACK
I was here first.
          (beat)
Stew . . .

                    STEW
I thought you were in--

                    JACK
I got bail.

                    STEW
Waste.

                    JACK
What happened to you?

                    STEW
I don't talk to thieves.

                    JACK
Ya sure don't mind dishin' dirt to reporters
or the cops.

                    STEW
That's my business.

                    JACK
Not when it's untrue and hurts people.

                    STEW
You got a convenient memory when it comes to
the truth.

                    JACK
You need to be honest with yourself about
what happened.

                          STEW
Whatever, man. I got shoppin' tuh do.

                          JACK
Really? We've known each other since high
school, and that's it!

                          STEW
I don't deal with embezzling brownnosers.

                          JACK
Brownnosers? Is that why you said those
things? Because I got a raise and you didn't?

                          STEW
I was the one that deserved it.

                          JACK
It was the manager's decision, not mine.

                          STEW
You kissed up to him.

                          JACK
I didn't even know I was going to get a raise
until it happened.

                          STEW
Right, thief.

                          JACK
I never took a thing from the store.

                          STEW
That's why you were charged, huh? Liar. Get
away.

        SOUND: A SHOPPING CART DISLODGES FROM
        ANOTHER SHOPPING CART.

                          JACK
You really have things mixed up.

                          STEW
In your dreams.

<u>SOUND: FOOTSTEPS START TO WHEEL A</u>
<u>SHOPPING CART OFF.</u>

                    JACK
Come on, Stew. This isn't right.
                    STEW
What?!
                    JACK
Take back the statements you made to the
media and the cops. You know they aren't
true.
                    STEW
Getcha hand off me.
                    JACK
I wasn't--
                    STEW
Do it again and I'll call Security.
                    JACK
You got it wrong.
                    STEW
Ya want everyone to hear about how you
assaulted me? Huh?!
          (beat)
Thought so, loser.

          <u>SOUND: FOOTSTEPS WHEEL A SHOPPING CART</u>
          <u>OFF.</u>

Let's take a look at how this scene is crafted. In terms of structure, it
begins with a chance meeting between Jack and Stew that leads to conflict.
The middle focuses on a growing dispute between the characters that gets
worse when Jack asks Stew to retract the harmful statements that he made
about him. The end has Stew threaten to make things worse for Jack if he
doesn't leave him alone. Jack's main obstacle in the scene is to ease the discord

between him and Stew in order to get Stew to retract the statements he made. His attempt to do so only aggravates Stew more, leading him to manipulate and strong-arm Jack. In that moment, Jack realizes that Stew is a serious threat and may create additional challenges for him going forward. In terms of character elements, it is revealed that Jack doesn't get riled easily in stressful situations. The scene also shows that Stew can be pushy and manipulative.

Scene Writing Checklist

After you write a scene, ask yourself the following questions:

- What is the main character's obstacle in the scene?
- What actions are the main character taking to combat that obstacle?
- What is the outcome of the main character's actions?
- Does the scene move the story forward? If so, how?
- What aspects of character are revealed during the scene?

If you find that the elements mentioned in the questions above are not included in the scene you have written, take time to add them. Once you have, your scene will be stronger and more dynamic because of it.

Chapter 6
Story World

The environment in which a story is set is comprised of certain rules, logic, and expectations, which collectively are known as the story's world. If it is normal for water to be purple, for characters not to be human, or for people to walk backward in a story, these elements need to be introduced early in the piece so the audience understands the world in which the story is set. Physical qualities and character attributes are just part of a story's world. There are several other elements that help to shape it as well.

Music

Music is a powerful component that contributes to the overall feel of a story's world. It establishes style, heightens mood, and may be used to transition from scene to scene. It can also be included in secondary ways, such as being heard on a radio or on a TV, or played live by a character or a band. If the company you work for has access to copyrighted material, you may include it in a script. Otherwise, it is best to suggest musical tone in one of the following ways:

- MUSIC: A HAUNTING, MECHANICAL MELODY PLAYS ON A TOY TRUMPET IN THE BACKGROUND.

- MUSIC: A MONOTONOUS, SINGLE-NOTE RHYTHM SLOWLY CRESCENDOS.

- MUSIC: A ROCK SONG IN THE STYLE OF THE ROLLING STONES BLASTS OUT OF A CAR RADIO.

These descriptions clearly communicate tone and intent. The more precise you are in the language you use to define music, the easier it will be for the production staff to incorporate the feel you are looking for into the final product.

Ambient Sound Library

Each location in a script contains sounds that are inherent to it and help define the story's world. These aural qualities are a vital part of making an environment feel authentic. No two settings have the same exact ambient sounds. How do you go about creating a unique sense of place? Start by observing the aural qualities that occur naturally in a location and write them down. To facilitate this process, consider setting up an ambient sound library. The library can be created in a spreadsheet or a table. List each place you want to document at the top of a separate column. Below each location, enter the sounds heard there. An example follows.

Living Room	Backyard Garden	Train Station Platform	Cafeteria	Country Road	Library
Gentle hum of a computer fan	Sparrows chirp	Footsteps	Medium roar of people chatting	Leaves rustle	Photocopier lid slams down
Ticking of a light timer	Bunny hops in the grass	Nearby chatter	Forks clink on plates	Cicadas chirp	Books plop onto a table
Intermittent air-conditioner fan blows, rumbles, or hums	Leaves blow lightly in the wind	Cars honk in the distance	Chairs scrape on tile floor	Birds flap their wings as they fly by	Patrons whisper
Flying insect taps on the outside of a window	Neighbors chatter in the distance	Clothes rustle	Cash register drawer opens/ shuts	Crackle of tires driving in the dirt	Door shuts in the distance
Intermittent creaking in a house	Airplane engine flies overhead	Train whistle blows	Trays slide across metal rails	Branches knock together	Water fountain motor hums
Muffled TV program in the background	Cars pass in the distance	Whish of passing trains	Mashed potatoes plop down on a glass plate	Bees buzz	Footsteps on carpet

(continued)

Living Room	Backyard Garden	Train Station Platform	Cafeteria	Country Road	Library
Animal feet patter on the roof	Putter of a lawn sprinkler	Trees rustle in the wind	Trash tossed into a garbage can	Distant farm machinery churns	Book slides out of a shelf
Wind rattles windows	Children ride by on bicycles	Train doors open/shut	Chewing or eating food	Water trickles in a stream	Library cart wheels squeak
Rain taps on the sidewalk outside	Children laugh in the distance	Train station platform creaks	Doors open and close	Deer trot	Book pages turn
Gurgle of an aquarium motor	Ice-cream truck jingle plays in the distance	Rain drizzles on the platform	Soda bottle dislodges from a vending machine	Breeze blows	Typing on a keyboard

Visit as many places as you can and document the sounds you hear there. Soon you will have a detailed library that enables you to bring your script to life in ways that guesswork cannot accomplish. Be sure to incorporate a light blend of ambient sounds into each scene you write.

Dialogue

Dialogue, which is discussed in more detail in chapter 4, is another tool that can help define a story's world. If the story you are telling is set in a fictitious place, visit towns that have a similar feel. If the script is set in a real town, go there. Listen for commonalities in how people talk. Do they use clipped, staccato phrases of one to two words? Do they have a certain rhythm to their speech? Do they use local slang? If so, jot these details down so you can use them to establish an overarching regional speech pattern that will make your story's setting distinct.

Time Period

Time period is a defining quality in the world of a story. It is established through era-appropriate dialogue, music, and other sounds. Be sure to research the period in which your story is set so you understand how people talk during that time. Select musical styles that are contemporary to the era. Consider other noises, such as those that emanate from technology used at that time as well. If your story is set on a train in 1872, see if any trains from that period are still active in living-history museums and take a ride on one. When you do, observe the sounds the train makes and how they affect the behavior of the passengers. Similarly, if you are creating a fictitious world, think about the aural qualities of various technologies native to that world and what adjustments characters need to make when dealing with them. Integrate that information subtly into your script. Doing so will give the piece an authentic feel to the period in which it is set.

Location

Audio dramatists need to be knowledgeable about the place in which their story is set. If it is a real location, research its history. If you are writing about a fictitious setting, create a history for it. Consider referencing period maps for actual locations or design your own for fictive ones to help you understand the landscape where your story occurs. Select character names that are related to the story's geography. The more you know about the setting, the more authentically you can portray it.

Since audio drama relies on sound to convey a sense of place, each time there is a change of scene, the new location needs to be set up for the listener. Even if a location has been used earlier in a script, it is important to reestablish it when it appears again. To set up a place, refer to your ambient sound library for specific sounds to use. If a scene occurs in a train station, people chatting, footsteps, doors opening, or muffled announcements over a loudspeaker may be heard. Include a few select sounds that instantly represent the location and complement the action that is occurring in the moment. Dialogue and music may be used to clarify location as well when needed.

Story World Example

Now that we have discussed how to create the world of a story and the unique locations within it, let's look at how these techniques come alive in scripted form. The following scene is based upon the character of Jack and his situation, which was set up in chapter 3.

Scene 1
(Jewelry store ambiance)

SOUND: LIGHT BACKGROUND CHATTER.

SOUND: A METAL NECKLACE DROPS INTO A VELVET SACK.

SOUND: A CINCH TIGHTENS.

SOUND: A VELVET SACK PLUNKS DOWN ON GLASS.

                    JACK
Nice choice, ma'am. I'll get your receipt.

SOUND: BOAT SHOE FOOTSTEPS OFF.

SOUND: RECEIPT PAPER TEARS.

SOUND: BOAT SHOE FOOTSTEPS APPROACH.

                    JACK (cont'd)
Here you are.

SOUND: RECEIPT PAPER RUSTLES.

                    JACK (cont'd)
We offer free cleaning on all gold jewelry purchased here.

                    FEMALE CUSTOMER
That's good to know.

                    JACK
Have a good night.

                    FEMALE CUSTOMER
You too.

SOUND: HIGH HEEL FOOTSTEPS OFF.

SOUND: A DOOR OPENS AND SHUTS.

SOUND: BUSINESS SHOE FOOTSTEPS APPROACH.

                    JACK'S BOSS
Nice work, Jack.

                                JACK
Thank you, sir.

                              JACK'S BOSS
I'm glad I moved you out front.

                                JACK
I hope it was all right to stay late.

                              JACK'S BOSS
For an order like that, definitely. Be sure to
put those rings on the back counter in the
vault before you go.

          SOUND: A PLASTIC BAG CONTAINING RINGS
          CLANKS AND RUSTLES.

                                JACK
I will, sir. See you next week.

          SOUND: A FEW BOAT SHOE FOOTSTEPS.

          SOUND: A VAULT DOOR OPENS.

          SOUND: A PLASTIC BAG CONTAINING RINGS
          CLANKS AND RUSTLES.

          SOUND: A VAULT DOOR SHUTS.

          SOUND: BOAT SHOE FOOTSTEPS.

          SOUND: BREAK AREA REFRIGERATOR HUM FADES
          UP.

          SOUND: BOAT SHOE FOOTSTEPS STOP.

          SOUND: COATS RUSTLE.

                            JACK (cont'd)
Hey, Stew. That's my coat.
                                STEW
Then take it.

                        JACK
Thanks.

        SOUND: A COAT RUSTLES.

                        STEW
That was my customer.

                        JACK
What are you talkin' about?

                        STEW
She looked at me when she came in.

                        JACK
I didn't know.

                        STEW
Yeah, right.

                        JACK
I didn't. If it's so important, make it clear
next time.

                        STEW
Believe me, I will.

                        JACK
What's with you lately?

                        STEW
Nothin'.

                        JACK
You sure?
            (beat)
Stew?

                        STEW
I gotta get back to work.

                        JACK
Okay.
            (beat)
Good night.

                              STEW
        Yeah, right.

              SOUND: DRESS SHOE FOOTSTEPS OFF.

    In this opening scene to Jack's story, notice how the location is set up
with a few key sounds that establish the jewelry store. There is a smooth aural
transition from the display counter to the vault to the break area. Distinct
sounds define each subsection of the store as Jack moves through them. His
behavior in each place provides insight into the world in which he works
and how he functions within it. Jack is respectful of customers and his boss
and knows how to back off from a tense situation with his peer in the hope
that the relationship will improve in the future. All of these qualities work
together to create the world of the story.

Helpful Hints: Five Ways to Create a Dynamic Story World

1. Research the history of the locations that appear in the script and
    insert details that accentuate the uniqueness of each setting.

2. Include mindsets and social norms that define how characters in the
    world behave and interact.

3. Suggest a mood within the musical underscoring of each scene,
    which gives a clear sense of the world's style and tone.

4. Feature innovations that are specific to the world and show how they
    affect the world's inhabitants.

5. Establish core qualities of the world early in the script that suggest
    there is more to the location than meets the eye, then reveal addi-
    tional attributes of the world as the story unfolds.

When you write a script, determine the most effective way to incorporate the elements discussed in this chapter. The more specific your choices, the more vibrant the story's world will be in the listener's mind.

Chapter 7
Story Structure

Structure is a process that is comprised of specific consistent elements. Consider a day in an average person's life, for example. Each morning, a person wakes up, goes about their day, and then goes to sleep at night. Some people may wake up and watch TV all day, others may wake up and work for twelve hours, still others may wake up and then nap in bed most of the day. Regardless of the variables that come into play, the basic process remains the same: people wake up, go about their day, and then sleep at night. That is the high-level structure that all variations must include. If you look closely at life, you'll find that most activities have some kind of high-level structure. Story is no different.

In order to use story structure effectively, you need to understand how it works. Every story has a beginning, a middle, and an end, which correspond to an act one, which is the setup; an act two, which depicts growing complications; and an act three, which is the resolution. At its highest level, the "hero's journey" structure contains eight essential components, which appear in a story in the following order:

Act One

- Opening status quo
- Inciting incident
- End of act one turning point

Act Two

- Mid–act two turning point
- Crisis

Act Three

- Obligatory scene
- Reversal
- Denouement

Let's take a closer look at each of these.

- Opening status quo. The moment in an audio drama when the main character is introduced in their daily environment. If their life is chaotic, the listener should hear them dealing with it. Likewise, if the protagonist's life is filled with boredom, the audience should hear how that affects them as well.
- Inciting incident. The event that takes the main character out of their everyday routine, gives them a goal to pursue, and starts them on their way to achieve it. (Note: There are several mounting obstacles the protagonist encounters after the inciting incident that lead to the next main structural moment.)

- <u>End of act one turning point.</u> A major obstacle that the protagonist faces at the end of act one. Once they come upon it, they can no longer give up their story goal and turn back. They are forced to push forward. (Note: The main character faces several challenges after this that lead up to the next major structural element.)
- <u>Mid–act two turning point.</u> A significant hurdle the protagonist encounters midway through act two. It increases the tension for the main character as they struggle to pursue their goal.
- <u>Crisis.</u> An unexpected challenge the protagonist faces, which occurs shortly after the mid–act two turning point.
- <u>Obligatory scene.</u> The main character's final battle, associated with reaching their goal.
- <u>Reversal.</u> The outcome of the obligatory scene. It answers the question, "Did the protagonist achieve or fail to achieve their story goal?"
- <u>Denouement.</u> The main character's new status quo. It shows how the story and its outcome have affected the protagonist's life.

Plot Types

In addition to the protagonist's primary journey, many audio dramas also contain subplots. These secondary journeys run concurrent with the main plot and provide insight into the protagonist. A subplot may affect the outcome of the primary story but does not have to. Secondary plots contain the same structural components that the main story does but move faster and are composed of fewer events. Feature-length audio dramas usually have one subplot, while serials may have none to a few. Each plot type is referred to by one of the following terms:

A plot. The main journey the protagonist goes on.

B plot. A secondary storyline that deals with part of the main character's life that is not directly related to their primary journey. It might be the pursuit of a love interest or a complication in their personal life that provides deeper insight into their character.

C plot. This type of substory is peppered lightly throughout a season of an audio-drama series. It adds intrigue or color, and may converge with the main story toward the end of the season but does not have to.

Story Opening Techniques

The way a story begins sets a tone and establishes expectations for everything that follows. In addition to the linear opening that many scripts use, there are other options that are important to be aware of. Each will enable you to reveal plot in unique and novel ways.

The first of these techniques is called a "precipitating event" or "catalytic moment." It starts the story off and appears to be unrelated to the main character's life. It is followed by the opening status quo. An example can be seen in detective stories that begin with a crime and then move to an investigator being assigned that crime to solve. Audience members will be intrigued by the "precipitating event" and will grow to understand its importance as the story unfolds.

Another option is a "pivotal story moment." It occurs at the beginning of a script and depicts part of a major dramatic event that directly relates to the main character, then cuts to the opening status quo. Similar to the "precipitating event," this technique creates intrigue and anticipation for the audience. Since listeners have heard a portion of the major dramatic event at the start of the story, they will want to stay tuned to learn what led up to it and how the story resolves afterward.

Alternate Story Structures

While the "hero's journey" is the predominant structure used to craft dramatic scripts, there are other methods that can be used as well. Each is based upon the "hero's journey" but uses it in different ways.

The "epic" story structure is a close relative of the hero's journey. It is exemplified by the classic Greek story *The Iliad* by Homer and features multiple storylines that occur at the same time. Each has its own protagonist and follows the "hero's journey" structure. All stories within a given piece contain a similar theme or occur in the same location. Soap operas are an example. They take place within a single town, industry, or family and track multiple main characters' journeys.

The "multiple point of view" structure revolves around several characters who recount their perspective on the same event. The story occurs at a specific moment in time. A group of characters individually speaks to the audience about a given situation. The story then flashes back to an earlier time and depicts each character's account of the situation. Once all characters have expressed their point of view on the event, the story returns to the present, where the various points of view are debated, and a final understanding of the situation is determined. Akira Kurosawa's film *Rashomon* is an example of this structure. It features characters testifying before a judging body about an event that occurred and then flashes back to dramatize their perspective on the event. After each character has given their account, the facts are discussed, and a conclusion is reached.

Storytelling Styles

There are a variety of styles that can be used to reveal key aspects of story in unique ways. Each operates under the "hero's journey" framework, yet provides the listener with a distinct experience. Methods include:

The Frame/Main Story. This approach involves a present-day frame story and a past main story that are interrelated. The frame story sets up a dramatic situation that transitions to the main story, which takes up the bulk of the storytelling landscape. When using the frame/main style, there needs to be a minimum of two frame scenes, one to open the story and another to conclude it. This category is derived from the "multiple point of view" structure yet does not include direct address or different perspectives on a past event.

Continuous Action. Scripts written in this style unfold in a single scene in real time, which means that the entire piece is told in one location without any jumps in time. Stories in this category tend to only have a main plot. B plots can be incorporated as long as they are integrated seamlessly into the storytelling without need for jumps in time.

Single Character. This type features a cast of one character who battles an obstacle on their own. The plot may jump through time or be continuous. Dialogue should sound realistic and drive the story forward. It should also come about as a result of the character responding to stimuli within the situation or environment in which they find themselves. Avoid having the character talk to themselves to reveal exposition or backstory.

High-Level Story Structure Example

Now that you have been introduced to the concept of story structure, let's look at how it works in a practical sense. The example that follows is the high-level structure for a thirty-minute audio-drama series pilot script. It is based upon the character of Jack and his situation that was introduced in chapter 3.

Opening status quo. A college student named Jack works hard in a jewelry store while receiving praise from his boss and envy from a peer.

Inciting incident. Jack is pulled over by a police officer, who finds stolen rings in Jack's trunk and arrests him. Jack vies to prove his innocence.

End of act one turning point. Jack calls his mother from jail, intending to ask for her assistance in getting an attorney and making bail, but Jack's stepfather blocks him from talking with her.

Mid–act two turning point. Jack befriends some fellow inmates who agree to help him in his pursuit to make bail yet set him up to be a scapegoat for their jailbreak instead.

Crisis. As Jack pursues a new tactic to get bail, he is charged with attempted jailbreak.

Obligatory scene. During a court hearing, Jack disputes the prosecution's claim that he is a flight risk and should not receive bail. He produces surveillance video that shows he was tricked into being the scapegoat for the other inmates' jailbreak.

Reversal. Jack is cleared of the jailbreak charge and granted bail.

Denouement. Jack reunites with his mother as theft charges loom and his disgruntled stepfather sighs in disapproval in the background.

The high-level structure of this story lays out the main events. Each element is written from the protagonist's point of view in an active manner that forces the protagonist to face obstacles. Using this technique will guarantee that the main character is the driver of the story. The inciting incident in this example establishes that Jack's primary goal is to make bail. He seeks help from his mother until his stepfather blocks it. Matters get worse when Jack finds himself the scapegoat for the other inmates' jailbreak. He uses his wits to prove he was set up to be a scapegoat and is not a flight risk. His actions enable him to make bail.

Helpful Hints: Five Ways to Create Exciting Plot Twists

1. Put the characters in jeopardy with no easy way out.
2. Determine what the worst thing that could happen is in a given moment and make it happen.
3. Reveal secrets that turn a situation on its ear.
4. Make a character confront their fears and phobias.
5. Insert a red herring that leads to an unexpected outcome.

If you word the high-level structure of your story in an active way, as seen in the example in this chapter, it will enable you to construct a solid foundation that you can build upon to create a dynamic, well-crafted audio-drama script.

Chapter 8
The Story Development Process

Crafting a story is a process that includes finding a story idea, outlining, writing the first draft of the script, and revising. Having a clear understanding of the steps it takes to develop a story will enable you to successfully write a script. Let's take a look at each step in the process.

Story Ideas

All stories begin as ideas. But where do you find ideas? For starters, look at photos, art, articles, dreams, mythology, general aspects of life, and your own experiences. Write your ideas down in a notebook or as individual documents on your computer. Give each idea a working title and note the date you created it. By doing this, you will have an idea bank you can reference when you are ready to start a new project.

There are two main types of story ideas. The first is character based. This means that the story grows out of qualities found within a character. If you have ideas for a character but don't have a story in which to feature them, explore their background. Determine what makes the character tick, who their friends are, what their outlook on life is, what challenges they have encountered, and what their goals are. Review the qualities outlined in chapter 3 to explore their character even further. Doing so will help you find story ideas that are authentic to the given character.

Plot-based ideas stem from action. There is a clear focus on what happens, which creates exciting dramatic moments; however, the characters tend to be functional and are solely there to drive the story forward. When developing a story in this category, it is important to spend time fleshing out the characters. Give them strengths, weaknesses, and depth. That will create an emotional connectivity between the characters and the story, which will make the characters more engaging and give the story more meaning overall.

Another technique for finding story ideas is called mapping. Mapping takes the main structure of a specific story, strips out the details, and allows the writer to populate that structure with their own characters, situation, and plot. If you map off of a popular story that resonates with an audience, there is a strong possibility the story you create will resonate with an audience as well. Writers have used this technique for centuries. The playwright William Shakespeare mapped off of the Bible, mythology, and other stories to create some of the plots used in his plays. You'd never know that from seeing them, though.

Let's walk through the mapping process. The first step is to select a story to map from. For this example, the fairy tale "Hansel and Gretel" as told by Jacob Grimm and Wilhelm Grimm will be used as source material.

Here is the original story.

Once a poor woodcutter and his wife lived deep in the woods with their children, Hansel and Gretel. When a famine hit, they weren't sure how they'd survive. The wife suggested to the woodcutter that if they got rid of the children, it would leave them with more to eat. The woodcutter wasn't sure, but his wife said it would work. Hansel and Gretel overheard their plan. Hansel snuck outside and filled his coat pocket with pebbles. The next morning, the woodcutter and his wife took the children deep into the forest. As they went, Hansel laid out a trail of pebbles. After a few hours, they emerged into a small clearing. The woodcutter and his wife told their children to rest there while they searched the nearby woods. They would come back for them later. Hansel and Gretel waited long into the night, but their parents never returned. The hours alone filled them with worry. They decided to follow the trail of pebbles back to the house, where they were reunited with their parents, who welcomed them in.

The children's return continued to present the woodcutter and his wife with the problem of having enough to eat. A few days later, the wife encouraged the woodcutter to again take the children deeper into the woods, so far that they would never find their way home and they would be rid of them. The children again overheard this conversation. Hansel tried to get some pebbles outside the house, but the door was locked so he couldn't. Early the next morning, the woodcutter and his wife gave the children a piece of bread to eat and then led them deeper into the woods than they had ever gone before. Hansel crumpled the bread in his pocket as they walked and left a trail of bread crumbs. The woodcutter and his wife eventually stopped to rest with their children and then told them they wanted to explore and would be back soon to bring them home.

The children waited for hours, but their parents never returned. By nightfall, Hansel and Gretel decided to follow the trail of crumbs back home. As they did, they discovered that the forest animals had eaten the trail, and they were stranded. Hansel and Gretel did the best they could to follow what they thought was the path home. They walked and walked and could not find their way home. They walked on for three more days and still had no luck. They were very hungry and growing weak. Soon, they heard a birdcall. They looked up and spotted a house made of bread and covered with cakes and candies. They were so hungry and excited that they went right up to the house and started eating some of the cake. Suddenly the door to the house opened, and an old woman came out, wanting to know who was eating her home. The children were terrified of her. The old woman soothed their fears and invited them inside. She fed them well and put them to bed. As the children slept, the old woman locked Hansel in a stable, then ordered Gretel to help her fatten up the animal that was locked in there. Once he was fat enough, the old woman would eat him. Gretel understood what she meant and was horrified. She had no choice but to do as the old witch commanded.

After four weeks of trying to fatten Hansel up—without success—the witch decided it was time to eat him. She got her oven to blazing and asked Gretel to creep in and see if it was hot enough. Gretel was suspicious and said she didn't know how to open the oven door. The old witch came over and opened it. In that moment, Gretel pushed the witch into the oven and shut the door, killing her. Gretel freed Hansel from the stable. They were thrilled to be rid of their nemesis. Hansel discovered the house was full of jewels. They each pocketed some and headed off.

After walking for some time, they came to a duck near a river. The duck let them ride on its back to the other side of the river. A short while later, Hansel and Gretel arrived at their father's farm. They found their father and learned that their mother had died. The children emptied the jewels from their pocket, saying that they would never have to go hungry again.[1]

Once you have a clear understanding of the main events in the story you select to map from, the next step is to identify the story's base structure. The primary story elements that are essential in the telling of "Hansel and Gretel" are outlined below.

- A trusted confidant leads the protagonist astray two times. The protagonist is left devastated.
- The protagonist wanders on the edge of destruction until they encounter someone who appears to be their salvation.
- That individual takes the protagonist in and seems to nurture them.
- It is revealed that the individual plans to use the protagonist for their own gain and then destroy them.
- The protagonist uses their wits to destroy the individual. In the process, the protagonist comes upon great valuables.
- The protagonist uses the valuables to create a better life for themselves.

The next step in the mapping process is to populate the structure above with specific characters and a situation. Mapping can be used for the main plot of a story, as the B plot, or for both. You can alter the base structure if it works better for the story you are crafting. Take some time to flesh out each character's background and give them traits that make them unique individuals. The example below is included to illustrate the mapping process.

Trust in Others
(based upon the structure of "Hansel and Gretel")

Situation: A young woman is tricked into being a drug runner for her employer. The employer betrays her when she gets wise to what he's involved in. The young woman seeks salvation from a friendly taxi driver who has ties to forced labor. He attempts to sell her off, but she resists and helps bring down the forced-labor ring in the process. The young woman receives a reward for her efforts and uses it to embark on a better life.

Characters:

Waitress – She is eighteen and has worked at a restaurant in New York City for six months. Prior to that, she lived in Elwood, Indiana. During her senior year in high school, her parents were killed in a train accident, which left her an orphan. Losing her parents hit her hard. After graduating, she decided to start life anew someplace else in the hope it would pick up her spirits. She had always wanted to live in New York City and decided to move there with her cat, Frisky. Since arriving, she has found making a living to be a struggle, but she likes the vibrance of the city and has vowed to make her life work there.

Fatherly restaurant co-owner – He is in his early forties and has owned the restaurant with his business partner for twenty years. He is kind to customers and likes to help new employees succeed. He feels the waitress will do better once she gains more experience. Honesty is important to him. He understands muscle is necessary sometimes in business situations. His business partner is good at that, so he lets him handle it. Everything must be on the up and up, though. He has a wife and a toddler son.

Dismissive restaurant co-owner – He is forty and manages the books for the restaurant. He has been engaged three times, but his roving eye has caused each relationship to end. He is attracted to women who are younger than he is and doesn't react well if he is rejected. He uses the restaurant to his advantage sometimes and feels that what his business partner doesn't know won't hurt him, as long as the restaurant makes a profit. This has led him to use the business as he sees fit, including as a front for under-the-table moneymaking ventures on occasion.

Taxi driver – Late twenties, attractive, friendly, and charismatic. He has been a taxi driver in New York City for seven years. He is a transplant from Chicago, where he liked to wheel and deal on the street until he became involved in an illegal scheme that went bad. When that occurred, he fled to New York and set up a life there. He quickly found work as a taxi driver and pursued alternate ways of making money, including loansharking and other nefarious endeavors. His philosophy is that if you're fool enough to be conned, you deserve what's coming to you. He shows no mercy. At the end of the day, it's all about the money.

Story Structure:

- A recently orphaned, high school graduate struggles to make a living as a waitress in a New York City restaurant. She seeks to advance herself in the industry in order to make it easier to get by in life. One of the restaurant's co-owners doesn't have the time of day for her while the other, a fatherly figure, says she is where she needs to be. Even so, she longs for more. The dismissive co-owner apologizes to the waitress for his behavior and says making deliveries will provide her with opportunity. She heads off to deliver an order, only to realize she has facilitated a drug purchase. The waitress discusses the situation with the fatherly co-owner, who swears he knew nothing about it and says he will talk with the dismissive co-owner. The dismissive co-owner claims he didn't know anything about it either. He pins the situation on the restaurant's chef who took the order and fires him. The waitress understands. Soon after, the dismissive co-owner asks the waitress to make another delivery. She does, only to have a gun put in her face for trying to pass off fake drugs. The purchaser tries to shoot her in retaliation for being defrauded. As the waitress flees, she overhears a radio broadcast that reveals that the dismissive co-owner has killed the fatherly co-owner over a dispute about illegal drugs. She is stunned.

- The enraged drug purchaser catches up to the waitress and fires at her. In desperation, the waitress runs over to an attractive taxi driver who is looking for a fare. She implores him to help her escape. He drives her away.
- The taxi driver gives the waitress refuge in his apartment and offers her a place to sleep.
- The next morning, the waitress awakes and overhears the driver in the adjoining room say he has another young one he's ready to sell into forced labor. He'll make the deal if the price is right. The waitress panics and tries to escape, but the driver comes in and stops her.
- Soon after, the waitress sits tied in the back of a taxi as the driver speeds along. He gloats about the money he's going to make off of her. The waitress manages to loosen some of her bonds and reaches her arms over the taxi driver's head in an effort to stop him. He fights her. She fights harder until the driver loses control of the car. The waitress removes her arms from around the driver as the car crashes; the driver is thrown through the windshield and to his death. The waitress is injured in the process but manages to pull herself from the car and flag down the police. She explains the situation and helps law enforcement shut down the forced-labor operation.
- The waitress is given an award for her assistance, which she uses to start a new life.

The example above uses the same structure as "Hansel and Gretel," yet has a different feel because of the specific characters, genre, and situation featured within it. These few steps are all that is needed to map a new story from existing source material.

Outlining

An outline is a tool that helps a writer develop a dynamic script in an efficient way. A writer may also share their outline with a producer so they can provide feedback and approve a story before the script is written. This saves time in the long run. There are several components that make up the outlining process. Let's take a look at each of them.

The first step is to select a story idea. A fully realized idea contains a main character who pursues a goal that is associated with a specific situation. If you are drawn to an idea that does not include all of these qualities, take some time to develop each of them.

The next phase is to write a three-paragraph summary of your story: the first paragraph introduces the elements found in act one, such as the main character, the situation, and their goal; the second paragraph highlights the act two components, including growing complications that the protagonist faces; and the third paragraph delves into the moments in act three that describing the main character's final battle to achieve their goal and the story's resolution. The intent of writing the summary is to set down a base journey for the protagonist to go on.

Once you have a brief narrative version of your story idea, it is time to identify the main structural points contained within it. An abbreviated version of the story structure components is included below for reference. Full details can be found in chapter 7.

Act One

- Opening status quo. (The moment in an audio drama when the main character is introduced in their daily life.)

- Inciting incident. (The event that takes the protagonist out of their everyday routine, gives them a goal to pursue, and starts them on their way to achieve it.)
- End of act one turning point. (A major obstacle the main character faces at the end of act one. Once they encounter it, they can no longer give up their story goal and turn back. They are forced to push forward.)

Act Two

- Mid–act two turning point. (A significant hurdle the protagonist comes upon midway through act two. It increases the tension for the main character as they struggle to pursue their goal.)
- Crisis. (An unexpected challenge the protagonist faces that occurs shortly after the mid–act two turning point.)

Act Three

- Obligatory scene. (The main character's final battle associated with reaching their goal.)
- Reversal. (The outcome of the obligatory scene. It answers the question, "Did the protagonist achieve or fail to achieve their story goal?")
- Denouement. (The main character's new status quo. It shows how the story and its outcome have affected the protagonist's life.)

Write down each of the high-level structural components that is mentioned above, such as:

- Opening status quo
- Inciting incident
- End of act one turning point

Review your three-paragraph summary and identify the elements that relate to a specific structural component. Write each element you identify next to the component it corresponds with. Once that has been done, review the story components that don't have an element next to them and create one. As you go about this process, ask yourself the following questions:

- What unexpected event could occur in this moment?
- How would that event ratchet up the stakes for the protagonist?
- How would that event force the main character to change or grow?
- How would that event turn the story in a fresh and innovative direction?

Exploring these questions will help you to create a unique story that is full of surprise twists. Take the time needed to thoroughly develop the high-level structure until it is dynamic and exciting. Be sure to delve into the history of each character and craft interesting, dimensional individuals to populate your story as well. Your script will only be as strong as the content you include in your outline. The following example from *Trust in Others* is provided as a practical example of how high-level story structure works.

Act One

- <u>Opening status quo.</u> A recently orphaned, high school graduate struggles to make a living as a waitress in a New York City restaurant. She seeks to advance herself in the industry in order to make it easier to get by in life. One co-owner doesn't have the time of day for her, while the other, a fatherly figure, says she is where she needs to be. Even so, she longs for more.
- <u>Inciting incident.</u> The dismissive co-owner apologizes to the waitress for his behavior and says making deliveries will provide her with

opportunity. She heads off to deliver an order, only to realize she has facilitated a drug purchase. The waitress discusses the situation with the fatherly co-owner, who swears he knew nothing about it and says he will talk with the dismissive co-owner.

- End of act one turning point. The dismissive co-owner asks the waitress to make another delivery. She does so, only to have a gun put in her face for trying to pass off fake drugs. The purchaser tries to shoot her in retaliation for being defrauded. As the waitress flees the enraged purchaser, she overhears a radio broadcast that reveals that the dismissive co-owner has killed the fatherly co-owner over a dispute about illegal drugs. The waitress dodges bullets as she struggles to escape the drug purchaser. In desperation, she runs over to an attractive taxi driver who is looking for a fare. She implores him to help her escape. He drives her away.

Act Two

- Mid–act two turning point. The waitress awakes in the taxi driver's apartment and overhears him in an adjacent room negotiating a deal to sell her into forced labor. The waitress panics. She tries to open the door and windows but discovers they are nailed shut.
- Crisis. The taxi driver enters the room in preparation to take the waitress off for sale. She tries to escape. He tackles her, then binds and gags her. She panics, unsure what to do.

Act Three

- Obligatory scene. The waitress sits tied in the back of a taxi as the driver speeds along. He gloats about the money he is going to make.

The waitress manages to loosen her ties, then reaches her arms over the driver's head attempting to disorient him, so he'll stop the car. They struggle until he loses control. The car crashes, thrusting the driver through the windshield and to his death.

- <u>Reversal.</u> The waitress gets banged up during the accident yet manages to pull herself from the car and flag down the police.
- <u>Denouement.</u> The waitress receives a reward for assisting the law in capturing the forced labor operator. She uses the money to start a new life.

The next step in the writing process is to create an outline. To do so, take the high-level structure of your story and flesh out the details that come between each major structural point. This is a working document that will evolve as you develop the story. Ideas may be added and then replaced with others until you find the perfect combination. If you aren't sure what goes in a particular section of the story, put a question mark there or state that a specific type of event is needed to bring the main character to the next structural point. With additional work, you will be able to find the needed plot aspects that address the missing moments in the story. An example from act one of the sample story *Trust in Others* is included below to illustrate the outlining process. This version of the story contains new details and character names.

Act One

- <u>Opening status quo.</u> Grace Preston, a recently orphaned, high school graduate, struggles to make a living as a waitress in a New York City restaurant. She was hired by Frank Tupput, the fatherly co-owner of the restaurant. The other co-owner, Kisch Stahl, finds Grace annoying and doesn't have the time of day for her. She tells Frank how she longs for more opportunity. He encourages her to focus on wait-ressing, where she will make more tips as she gains experience. She appreciates his support, though it doesn't change her desire to learn more about the industry. With no hope for advancement, Grace continues her daily work.

- <u>Inciting incident.</u> Grace finds Kisch in a stressed-out mood and offers him supportive words. He growls at her and her naivety about life. She says she's going to find a way to do more at the restaurant someday and advance herself. Kisch perks up and apologizes for his behavior to date. He encourages her to make deliveries. That will give her more insight into the business. She eagerly agrees to the opportunity. Kisch says it is just between them. When an order is ready, Grace heads off to deliver it.

- Grace delivers the restaurant order. In the process, she realizes she has facilitated a drug purchase. She is concerned.

- Grace returns to the restaurant and approaches Kisch about the delivery. He blows her off, saying that every customer she meets won't be nice. If she wants to get ahead in the business, she needs to get a thicker skin or find another line of work. She thinks that's crazy. He fires her.

- As Grace gathers her belongings, she sees Frank and discusses her delivery experience with him. He swears he knew nothing about the drugs and says he will talk with Kisch.

- Frank and Kisch discuss Grace's delivery experience as she looks on. Grace gets Kisch to realize that he didn't listen to her or give her a chance. He doesn't know how drugs could be mixed in with an order but will look into it. Frank is annoyed by Kisch's behavior and assures Grace she can continue to work at the restaurant. Grace is glad.

- Grace asks people in the kitchen about the order she was sent to deliver and finds some drugs in the chef's coat in the process.

- Grace asks the chef about the order. He claims it was just an average order.

- Grace finds a paper in the trash that contains the phone number associated with the order. She goes to the restaurant's office and finds it vacant. Since no one is around, she decides to access the restaurant's computer. While scrolling through business records, Grace discovers that the phone number she found has several orders associated with it.

- Grace tries to open the desk drawer while looking for a pencil. The drawer is locked. Kisch comes in and asks what she is doing. She explains and then tells him what she found out about the chef. Kisch is unhappy to hear this. He says he is still investigating the situation and will get to the bottom of it.

- Grace arrives home to her small apartment after work. She goes through the mail, finding several bills and a letter threatening eviction if she doesn't pay her back rent soon. She pets her cat, Frisky, and looks out the window, unsure what to do.

- The next day, Kisch apologizes to Grace for not believing her. He informs her that he discovered that the chef was using food deliveries for his personal drug-running business. He was fired. Kisch isn't going to the police because he is concerned any negative publicity could hurt the business. Grace is glad he believes her and hopes for more opportunity to advance herself in the restaurant business. He agrees.

- End of act one turning point. A few days later, Kisch offers Grace another opportunity to make a food delivery. She agrees to go. When she makes the delivery, the purchaser pulls a gun on her for trying to pass off fake drugs. She swears she knew nothing about it. The purchaser shoots at her in retaliation for being defrauded. She ducks, then flees, as the enraged purchaser chases her. In the process, Grace runs past a car that blasts its radio. She overhears a radio broadcast announce that Kisch has killed Frank over a dispute when Frank discovered Kisch was secretly running an illegal drug business out of their restaurant. Grace continues to dodge bullets while struggling to escape from the drug purchaser. As she flees in desperation, she spots an attractive taxi driver named Luke who is looking for his next fare. She implores him to help her escape. They get in the taxi and drive off.

The sample outline above fleshes out the story. It contains a clear journey for the protagonist to go on, insight into the main character, and obstacles for her to pursue along the way. It is a working document that enables you to develop the story. Once you have worked out the details of the story, you are ready to move on.

The last step in the outlining process is to create a scene breakdown. This document evolves out of the outline and consists of a synopsis for each scene that will be in the script. It should include as little or as much information as you need to write the script. An example from act one of *Trust in Others* is included below as a guide.

Trust in Others
(Scene Breakdown)

Act One
SCENE 1 (Opening status quo)
Grace Preston, a recently orphaned, high school graduate, struggles to make a living as a waitress in a New York City restaurant. She was hired by Frank

Tupput, the fatherly co-owner of the restaurant. The other co-owner, Kisch Stahl, finds Grace annoying and doesn't have the time of day for her. She tells Frank how she longs for more opportunity. He encourages her to focus on waitressing, saying she will make more tips as she gains experience. With no hope for advancement, Grace continues her daily work.

SCENE 2 (Inciting incident)

Grace finds Kisch in a stressed-out mood and offers him supportive words. He growls at her and her naivety about life. She says she's going to find a way to do more at the restaurant someday. All she needs is a chance. Kisch perks up and apologizes for his behavior to date. He encourages her to make deliveries. That will give her more insight into the business. She eagerly agrees to the opportunity. Kisch says it is just between them. When an order is ready, Grace heads off to deliver it.

SCENE 3

Grace delivers the restaurant order to a customer. In the process, she realizes that she has facilitated a drug purchase.

SCENE 4

Grace returns to the restaurant and approaches Kisch with concern about the delivery. He refuses to listen, telling her that all customers aren't nice. If she wants to get ahead in the business, she needs to get a thicker skin or find another line of work. She thinks that's crazy. He fires her.

SCENE 5

As Grace gathers her personal belongings, she sees Frank and discusses her delivery experience with him. He swears he knew nothing about the drugs and says he will talk with Kisch.

SCENE 6

Frank and Kisch discuss Grace's delivery experience while she looks on. Grace gets Kisch to realize that he didn't give her a chance to explain that drugs were involved. He doesn't know how drugs could have been mixed in with the order but will look into it. Frank is annoyed by Kisch's behavior and assures Grace she can stay on. Grace is glad.

SCENE 7

Grace asks people in the kitchen about the order she delivered and finds some drugs in the chef's coat in the process.

SCENE 8

Grace asks the chef about the order. He claims it was just an average order.

SCENE 9

Grace finds a paper in the trash with the phone number and address of the order on it.

SCENE 10

When Kisch steps away from doing some data entry at his desk, Grace accesses his computer and looks up the phone number on the delivery order. She discovers that orders have been associated with that phone number regularly for over a month. Grace searches for a pen to write down the information. Kisch returns and asks what she is doing. She tells him what she has found out about the chef and the purchaser of the order. Kisch is unhappy to hear this. He says he is still investigating the situation and will get to the bottom of it.

SCENE 11

Grace arrives home to her small apartment after work. She goes through the mail, finding several bills and a letter threatening eviction if she doesn't pay her back rent soon. She pets her cat, Frisky, and looks out the window, unsure what to do.

SCENE 12

The next day, Kisch apologizes to Grace for not believing her about the order she delivered. He tells her that he recently discovered that the chef was using deliveries for his personal drug-running business. He was fired. Kisch isn't going to the police because he is concerned that potential negative publicity relating to the matter could hurt the business. Grace is glad he believes her and hopes for more opportunity to advance herself in the restaurant business. Kisch agrees.

SCENE 13

A few days later, Kisch offers Grace another opportunity to make a food delivery. She agrees to go.

SCENE 14 (End of act one turning point)

Grace walks into a run-down tenement with spaced-out people lying in the halls. She delivers the order, only to have the purchaser pull a gun on her for trying to pass off fake drugs. She swears she knew nothing about it. The purchaser shoots at her in retaliation for being defrauded. She darts off as the purchaser pursues her, shooting at her. In the process, she runs past a car that blasts its radio. She overhears a news broadcast announce that Kisch has killed Frank over a dispute when Frank found Kisch was secretly running an illicit drug business out of their restaurant. Grace is surprised. She continues to dodge bullets while struggling to escape from the purchaser. As she flees in desperation, she spots an attractive man named Luke standing outside a taxi in the distance. He is getting some sun while looking for his next fare. Grace runs up and implores him to help her escape. They get in his taxi and drive off.

The story may continue to evolve as you write the scene breakdown as seen in the example above. Once the breakdown has been completed, you are ready to write the script.

The First Draft

Writing the first draft of a script is your opportunity to bring the story to life. You developed an outline and characters during the planning stage. Now is your chance to enjoy writing the script. I recommend writing the entire draft straight through from beginning to end without editing. You will have time to focus on revisions later.

If you want to write the initial draft in a timely manner, set up a writing schedule. To do so, first quantify how much work there is to do. This is done by noting how many scenes are in the scene breakdown. Next, determine how much you plan to write each day. If there are thirty scenes in the breakdown and you write one a day, it will take you a month to complete the initial draft. Likewise, if you write five scenes a day, you will finish the first draft in six days. Take time to create a schedule that works for you. Be sure to factor in the days in which you will not be able to write.

Script Revision

Once the initial draft of the script has been written, you are ready for the next phase, revision. This begins by reading the script. As you do, take note of the strengths and weaknesses of the draft. Ask yourself, did it come out as you had planned? Are all aspects of the plot dramatized to their full potential? Are each character's traits clearly established? Once you have completed this assessment, you will be ready to implement the changes you noted.

The next step in the revision process involves character dialogue. Open the character speech dictionary and review each character's lines one character at a time. When you come upon a unique phrase or pattern in a character's voice, add it to their section of the speech dictionary. Once that has been completed, review all of the character's dialogue and flesh out their voice according to the entries in the speech dictionary. As you define their voice in the script, you may discover additional nuances. Be sure to add them to the character speech dictionary. Repeat this process for each character who appears in the script.

You are now ready to focus on the script's soundscape. The first step is to open the ambient sound library you created earlier. Review the sounds in the script against a comparable location in your sound library. Incorporate unique, yet essential sounds into each scene that create a visceral aural experience for the listener. Don't overdo it. Use a concise blend of sounds that evoke a sense of place and create dramatic movement within each scene.

Once you have revised the script on your own, it is important to get feedback. Ask a fellow audio dramatist or an audio-drama writing group to review your script. (See chapter 13 for information on writing groups.) When a fellow writer is ready to give feedback, it is your opportunity to see how they experienced the script. The most important thing to do is listen and take notes. You can ask questions if clarity is needed, but try not to defend your work. Doing so may prevent your fellow writers from providing suggestions that could help improve your script.

After you receive feedback, take a few days off. The break will give you distance from the project, which will in turn enable you to gain perspective on the feedback you received. When you are ready to resume work, go through the feedback. If at least two people have a similar note, it is something you should address when revising the script. That doesn't mean if only one person mentioned something you shouldn't take it seriously. Assess all feedback and determine which notes you want to pursue.

Once you have reviewed the feedback, you are ready to begin the rewrite process. The first step is to compile all aspects you want to work on into a single document. Development points associated with act one of *Trust in Others* will be used as an example in the process that follows. Development notes include:

- Distinction between the two drug customers is needed. In the current draft, they feel like the same person. Make them unique individuals.

- Flesh out Grace's character so she has depth.
- Clarify why Kisch treats Grace in a dismissive manner.

The next step is to select the first note to work on. Once you decide, outline everything in the script that is associated with that layer of the story. Be sure to include scene numbers. They will help you identify where each moment of that layer occurs. An example follows.

- <u>Clarify why Kisch treats Grace harshly.</u>
  - <u>Scene 1 (Opening status quo):</u> Grace Preston, a recently orphaned, high school graduate, struggles to make a living as a waitress in a New York City restaurant. She was hired by Frank Tupput, the fatherly co-owner of the restaurant. The other co-owner, Kisch Stahl, finds Grace annoying and doesn't have the time of day for her. She tells Frank how she longs for more opportunity. He encourages her to focus on waitressing, saying she will make more tips as she gains experience. With no hope for advancement, Grace continues her daily work.
  - <u>Scene 2 (Inciting incident):</u> Grace finds Kisch in a stressed-out mood and offers him supportive words. He growls at her and her naivety about life. She says she's going to find a way to do more at the restaurant someday. All she needs is a chance. Kisch perks up and apologizes for his behavior to date. He encourages her to make deliveries. That will give her insight into the business. She eagerly agrees to the opportunity. Kisch says it's just between them. When an order is ready, Grace heads off to deliver it.
  - <u>Scene 4:</u> Grace returns to the restaurant and approaches Kisch with concern about the delivery. He refuses to listen, telling her that all customers aren't nice. If she wants to get ahead in the

business, she needs to get a thicker skin or find another line of work. She thinks that's crazy. He fires her.

- Scene 5: As Grace gathers her personal belongings, she sees Frank and discusses her delivery experience with him. He swears he knew nothing about the drugs and says he will talk with Kisch.

- Scene 6: Frank and Kisch discuss Grace's delivery experience while she looks on. Grace gets Kisch to realize that he didn't give her a chance to explain that drugs were involved. He doesn't know how drugs could have been mixed in with the order but will look into it. Frank is annoyed by Kisch's behavior and assures Grace she can stay on. Grace is glad.

- Scene 7: Grace asks people in the kitchen about the order she delivered and finds some drugs in the chef's coat in the process.

- Scene 10: When Kisch steps away from doing some data entry at his desk, Grace accesses his computer and looks up the phone number on the delivery order. She discovers that orders have been associated with that phone number regularly for over a month. Grace searches for a pen to write down the information she found on the computer. Kisch returns and asks what she is doing. She tells him what she has found out about the chef and the purchaser of the order. Kisch is unhappy to hear this. He says he is still investigating the situation and will get to the bottom of it.

- Scene 11: Grace arrives home to her small apartment after work. She goes through the mail, finding several bills and a letter threatening eviction if she doesn't pay her back rent soon. She pets her cat, Frisky, and looks out the window, unsure what to do.

- Scene 12: The next day, Kisch apologizes to Grace for not believing her about the order she delivered. He tells her that he recently discovered that the chef was using deliveries for his personal drug-running business. He was fired. Kisch isn't going to the police because he is concerned that potential publicity relating to the matter could hurt the business. Grace is glad he believes her and hopes for more opportunity to advance herself in the restaurant business. Kisch agrees.

- ○ <u>Scene 13</u>: A few days later, Kisch offers Grace another opportunity to make a food delivery. She agrees to go.
- ○ <u>Scene 14 (End of act one turning point)</u>: Grace walks into a run-down tenement with spaced-out people lying in the halls. She delivers the order, only to have the purchaser pull a gun on her for trying to pass off fake drugs. She swears she knew nothing about it. The purchaser shoots at her in retaliation for being defrauded. She darts off as the purchaser pursues her, shooting at her. In the process, she runs past a car that blasts its radio. She overhears a news broadcast announce that Kisch has killed Frank over a dispute when Frank found Kisch was secretly running an illicit drug business out of their restaurant. Grace is surprised. She continues to dodge bullets while struggling to escape from the purchaser. As she flees in desperation, she spots an attractive man named Luke standing outside of a taxi in the distance. He is getting some sun while looking for his next fare. Grace runs up and implores him to help her escape. They get in his taxi and drive off.

After identifying the scenes that need to be looked at, the next step is to determine why Kisch doesn't like Grace. Revise Kisch's character background to include that he is more than twenty years older than Grace. He thinks highly of himself and is used to having his way with women. He is attracted to Grace. She politely hints that she is not interested. Kisch is hurt by Grace's lack of interest in him. Now that we know why he treats her the way he does, it needs to be incorporated into the outline. Determine what exchanges Grace and Kisch have regarding his attraction and then incorporate them into the layer of the outline as follows.

- Clarify why Kisch treats Grace harshly.
  - Scene 1 (Opening status quo): Add that when Grace works at the restaurant, Kisch flirts with her. She doesn't react. Kisch becomes annoyed and blows her off when she approaches him about work. Grace moves on to discuss advancement opportunities with Frank, who encourages her to stay where she is.
  - Scene 2 (Inciting incident): After Kisch takes Grace's concern for him as attraction, add that she subtly clarifies that her concern is nothing more than general compassion for a fellow human being. That's all. Kisch acts coolly toward her. That is followed by Grace asking for a new opportunity at the restaurant. Kisch offers her the delivery work. She is interested and takes it.
  - Scene 4: Add that when Grace tells Kisch about her delivery experience, he says he gave her an opportunity. Since she can't handle it and doesn't appreciate what he's done for her, she is fired.
  - Scene 5: Add that Grace briefly mentions the advances Kisch made to her when she tells Frank about the delivery and her being fired. Frank swears he knew nothing about any of it. He says he will talk with Kisch.
  - Scene 6: When Frank and Kisch discuss Grace's delivery, add that Grace gets Kisch to realize that she likes him as a boss and that he didn't give her a chance in her new role. Kisch doesn't know how there could be such a misunderstanding between

them or a mix-up with an order like that. Frank is annoyed by Kisch's behavior and agrees to let Grace stay on. She is glad.

- ○ Scene 12: When Kisch apologizes to Grace for not believing her about the delivery, add a subtle hint that he likes her. Grace doesn't react to it. Kisch has a momentary reaction of displeasure and then refocuses on their work.
- ○ Scene 14 (End of act one turning point): After Grace overhears the news broadcast about Kisch killing Frank after his drug business was exposed, add that Grace realizes her rejection of Kisch has led him to send her on the current delivery in an attempt to hurt her again.

The sample outline above only includes aspects that relate to the specific development note. The rest of the scene occurs as it does in the original script. If you find no changes are needed to a scene during this process, delete the scene from the outline as in the example above. Once you have addressed all revisions through the replotting process, you are ready to implement your changes into the script. I recommend working on one note or story layer at a time.

After you revise the entire script, seek out additional feedback from writing colleagues and revise the script again as needed. Repeat the feedback/revision process until you have made the script the best that you can. Once you have, you are ready to start submitting it to audio-drama production companies.

Chapter 9
Adaptation

Adaptation is the transfer of a story from one medium to another. Some of the most popular audio dramas enjoyed by audiences today are adapted from novels, short stories, and plays. Having the skill to craft an adaptation will make you more marketable as an audio dramatist. Short stories and novels use the five senses to communicate story. Audio drama uses one sense: sound. Because of this, if you adapt a short story or novel into an audio drama, some elements of the original story may need to be depicted differently in order to convey their meaning effectively in the new medium.

The story that is being adapted is considered source material for the adaptation. When a rights holder licenses their story for an audio adaptation, they may place limitations on what can be done. If that is not the case, the audio dramatist is free to use the source material as they choose. This means that you may change some characters, delete some characters, add new characters, or cut or alter aspects of the plot as you see fit in order to craft the most effective and dynamic script. There are two main types of adaptations: "close to the book" and liberal. Let's take a look at how each works.

A close to the book adaptation retains most of the details found in the source material. This means that it follows the plot closely and depicts the characters in a way that captures their essence in the original story. Audio dramatists often use portions of dialogue from the source material in their script to further this purpose. The combination of these qualities helps to create a story world that is similar to that of the original work.

Let's look at an approach to do a close adaptation of Jules Verne's novel *Mysterious Island*. Chapter 1 of the story opens with several characters caught in a hot-air balloon disaster over the ocean. The audience knows little about each character. Chapter 2 delves into the backstory for the characters in the balloon and explains what led them to get in it. Chapter 3 resumes the balloon disaster and its crash on the coast of a deserted island. This structure makes an exciting setup for a novel. An audio-drama audience needs to be kept engaged with the forward progression of the story at all times. Opening the script with a balloon chase only to cut away to discuss backstory and then return to the balloon chase lessens the dramatic impact of the script. To keep the story building and introduce the characters at the same time, an adaptation of *Mysterious Island* could begin with a dramatic depiction of what led the characters to the balloon, as discussed in chapter 2 of the book. From there, the adaptation could move to the balloon escape in chapter 1 and then to chapter 3, where the balloon crash lands on a deserted island. This is still considered a close to the book adaptation, but the modifications provide insight into who the main characters are before they become involved in the balloon escape and subsequent crash.

A liberal adaptation molds the source material to tell a story that the audio dramatist wants to tell. The process starts with the writer selecting a universal premise about life that can be explored in the adaptation. The characters may be different, the time and setting may not be the same, and the events depicted in the adaptation may have a different meaning than they do in the source material. Despite these changes, the adaptation still resembles the original story, which makes it a liberal adaptation and not mapping.

Let's go over an example of how to create a liberal adaptation of Jules Verne's *Mysterious Island*. The script could open in outer space with an astronaut desperately hanging on to the outside of a spaceship during a burst of solar winds. The strong gust rips the astronaut off of the ship and thrusts them onto the shore of a strange planet polluted with by-products from earth. They struggle to survive alone while trying to overcome the pollution and searching for a way to return to earth. This concept uses the same events as the original story, yet it changes the setting and focuses the theme on environmentalism, which demonstrates how a writer can imbue an adaptation with deep meaning that might only be touched upon in the original story.

Copyright

When you are searching for material to adapt, there are several different types of sources to consider. These include the public domain, copyrighted material, articles, and even your own work. Understanding each will help you choose which category will work best for you.

Public Domain

Stories in the public domain are free of copyright restrictions. This means that they can be used without the need to seek permission or compensate anyone. As of the writing of this book, stories published in the United States before 1928 fall into this category, along with some novels and story magazines from the 1930s to the 1960s whose copyright has lapsed. The website Project Gutenberg contains the full text for thousands of stories that are in the public domain. While it is a robust resource, it is advisable to independently confirm that a story is in the public domain before using it as source material for an audio-drama adaptation.

Copyrighted Material

If you are interested in adapting a story or novel that has an active copyright, meaning that the author or rights holder is living or died within the last seventy years, you will need to get written permission before using their material. In doing so, the rights holder may charge you a fee or establish a specific amount of time to grant you the right to adapt their story and seek production. Once that time expires, the rights to their story will revert back to them. While you will own the adaptation at that point, you will not be able to do anything with it without the underlying rights holder's permission. You will need to sign an agreement with them that establishes these terms. It is essential to obtain permission before adapting a story that has an active copyright. If you don't, you run the risk of adapting the story only to find out that the rights holder won't grant you permission to use their work.

Articles

Articles that appear in newspapers, magazines, and websites are another source of material to adapt. Most will have a copyright. You will need to get clearance from the rights holder before using their work. The exception to this rule occurs when a true account has been published broadly. Since the facts of the account are widely known in the public sphere, they are considered general information. Copyright does not apply to this type of information—only the specific language in which the information is conveyed.

Your Own Work

If you write stage plays, original TV scripts, screenplays, short stories, or novels, adapting them into audio dramas will open up a new market for your work. Stage plays, which tend to be situationally based and dialogue driven, are the easiest to adapt. TV scripts and screenplays require reimagining the visual elements of the story so they can be communicated clearly and authentically in audio drama. Adapting a story in this category will give it the potential to connect with a new audience.

Verifying Rights

Occasionally, a story may be in the public domain, but elements of it are protected as trademarks, which follow a different set of rules than copyrights do. If you select a story to adapt that falls into this category, be sure to verify that there are no trademarks related to the characters, title, or other attributes of the story. A simple, free search can be conducted at Trademarkia.com or through the United States Patent and Trademark Office website. If an element within the story you selected is trademarked, you will need to get permission from the trademark holder before using that component in your adaptation.

Adaptation Techniques

Once you have selected a story, you are ready to begin the adaptation process. There are several techniques from which to choose. Each is discussed below. Review the methods carefully and choose the one that works best for you.

Outlining

Outlining is a structured approach to adaptation. The first step is to read the story so you understand the characters, the plot, and the storytelling style.

Take note of aspects that appear challenging to adapt. These may include extensive use of description or exposition, lack of substantial plot, or internal stories that deal with a character's thoughts and not actions. Later in the process, you can decide how best to handle these aspects.

Determine the length of the script. Standard running times include ten-minute shorts, thirty-minute episodes, and full-length pieces. It all depends upon what you are looking to do with the story and the amount of time in which you want to tell it.

The next step is to decide whether you are creating a close to the book or liberal adaptation. Reflect on the qualities within the story and determine what meaning you want the audience to glean from listening to the production. Incorporate that meaning into the adaptation.

Now that you have defined a concept for the adaptation, you are ready to begin the outline. Start by creating a list of the story beats that relate to the theme you are exploring in your telling of the story. Be sure to clearly summarize the plot points you intend to include in the adaptation. Consider referencing page numbers in the source material or pasting parts of the text into your outline so you can refer to them when drafting the script. Next, review the components that appear challenging to adapt and determine whether they should be included or cut. Once this has been accomplished, revise the outline until it is concise, well-structured, and engaging. At that point, you will be ready to write the script.

The Action-Driven Technique

The action-driven technique is an in-the-moment method of adapting a story into an audio-drama script. There are two approaches to choose from: read the source material through once to get an understanding of the plot or read the story as you adapt it. The action-driven technique may be used for close to the book or liberal adaptations.

Begin the adaptation by identifying the protagonist and what their story goal is. Once these elements have been established, adapt the text while you read it, focusing on dramatizing the obstacles the protagonist faces as they pursue their goal. Everything else in the source material can be left out. If the original story contains a large cast, consider cutting out characters or combining multiple characters into a single composite character. Each of these steps is done in the moment as you adapt the story into an audio play.

Once you have completed the initial draft of the adaptation, read through it. Take note of any holes in the plot and verify that your main character is consistently pursuing their goal. A brief amount of outlining may be needed at this point to fix any noted issues and flesh out characters. Make sure the script is the length you were aiming for. Revise it as needed until you have a fully realized draft that encompasses the story you want to tell.

Converting Short-Form Source Material into Long Form

The length of an original story does not dictate the running time of an adaptation of it. By following a few key steps, it is possible to take a short story and expand it into a thirty-minute or full-length audio drama. There are two main approaches you can use to do so.

The first method involves a process called expansion. Once you have established the protagonist and their story goal, identify areas in the original story that summarize events or large passages of time instead of actively depicting them. Make these moments pivotal to the main character's journey and then dramatize them. This can be done by using the outline or in-the-moment adaptation technique.

Let's look at an excerpt from Philip K. Dick's short story "Beyond the Door" to explore the expansion technique. The story centers around a young woman named Doris who feels unappreciated by her husband, Larry. He gives her a cuckoo clock to keep her company while he works day and night. The clock becomes Doris's main source of companionship. Larry grows to despise it. Doris feels unappreciated and eventually leaves him. At that moment in the story, the text says the following:

> In the weeks that followed after Doris left, Larry and the cuckoo clock got along even worse than before. For one thing, the cuckoo stayed inside most of the time, sometimes even at twelve o'clock when he should have been busiest. And if he did come out at all he usually spoke only once or twice, never the correct number of times. And there was a sullen, uncooperative note in his voice, a jarring sound that made Larry uneasy and a little angry.
>
> But he kept the clock wound, because the house was very still and quiet and it got on his nerves not to hear someone running around, talking and dropping things. And even the whirring of a clock sounded good to him.[1]

This is an example of a passage of time. The events are summarized and not fully depicted. As a prose writing technique, it is effective in moving the story along quickly, yet it leaves out moment-by-moment details. To expand this section into a fully realized dramatic event in an adaptation, look at each action in the source material. For example, the first sentence in the excerpt above states:

> In the weeks that followed after Doris left, Larry and the cuckoo clock got along even worse than before.[2]

This line suggests that Doris leaves Larry; however, the moment of her departure is not depicted. The next part of the sentence states that Larry's frustration with the clock grew over time. These are important elements to dramatize for the audience. One approach is to write a progression of scenes that depicts Doris leaving and then Larry encouraging the bird to come out of the clock. It refuses to each time until Larry's frustration with the cuckoo clock makes him erupt in anger. Dramatizing these moments expands the story in a manner that is authentic to the original text and clarifies how each aspect actually occurred.

The second method to transform a short story into a longer-form adaptation involves dramatizing aspects associated with the protagonist that are hinted at or left out of the source material. Once you identify these moments, determine the most effective way to expand each of them so it provides deeper insight into the main character's personality.

Let's look at the opening of "Beyond the Door" to better understand how aspects of the story can be extended to flesh out the protagonist's character. The original text states:

> THAT NIGHT at the dinner table he brought it out and set it down beside her plate. Doris stared at it, her hand to her mouth. "My God, what is it?" She looked up at him, bright-eyed.
>
> "Well, open it."
>
> Doris tore the ribbon and paper from the square package with her sharp nails, her bosom rising and falling. Larry stood watching her as she lifted the lid. He lit a cigarette and leaned against the wall.
>
> "A cuckoo clock!" Doris cried. "A real old cuckoo clock like my mother had." She turned the clock over and over. "Just like my mother had, when Pete was still alive." Her eyes sparkled with tears.[3]

These initial paragraphs introduce the reader to the primary characters, Doris and Larry, yet little is known about either of them. Lack of detail provides the audio dramatist with the opportunity to flesh out the characters and their relationship in the adaptation. To get started, answer the following questions:

- Who is the protagonist?
- What is the dynamic between the two characters?
- Where do Doris and Larry live?
- What does Doris do when Larry is away?

Armed with the answers to these questions, review the source material. It begins with Larry giving Doris the clock. That event takes Doris out of the opening status quo and sets her on a journey to have a meaningful relationship. If you expand upon the opening moments of the story in the adaptation, you can develop who the characters are and how their world operates. Let's look at a scripted example of how this can be done.

<u>Scene 1</u>
(Kitchen ambiance)

<u>SOUND: STEW BOILS.</u>

<u>SOUND: A DOOR SHUTS.</u>

LARRY
(distant)
Hey, hon. I'm home.

DORIS
(calling out)
Hi, Larry. I'm in the kitchen.

<u>SOUND: FOOTSTEPS APPROACH.</u>

LARRY
What's for grub?

DORIS
Lamb stew.

LARRY
Again?

                              DORIS
It's what they had on special at the
butcher's. If you'd let me go out and work--

                              LARRY
We've been over that.

                              DORIS
Let's go over it again while we eat.

                              LARRY
Can't. Boss wants me there early tonight.

                              DORIS
I never get to see you anymore. If you're not
working at the mill, you're scarfing down food
and dashing out the door to that second job.

                              LARRY
We need the money, hon.

                              DORIS
It would be easier if I pitched in.

                              LARRY
How? You got fired from the last three jobs
you had.

                              DORIS
Only because you kept coming there and
arguing with me. You gotta keep it down in
restaurants. Customers don't like all that
noise. That's what the managers told me. And
that's what got me fired.

                              LARRY
All your squawking has kept me from eating.
Now I'm gonna be late for work.
                    (kisses her)
I'll see you tonight.

                              DORIS
In your dreams.

                              LARRY
What?

                    DORIS
You're comin' in at eleven thirty like usual,
right?

                    LARRY
So?

                    DORIS
I'll be asleep by then, so you can see me in
your dreams.

                    LARRY
Keep me here talking like this, and I won't
have a job to go to no more.

                    DORIS
At least then we'll have some time together.

                    LARRY
Yeah, but we'll be in the poorhouse.

                    DORIS
We couldn't be much poorer than we are now.
Look at this kitchen. An ancient stove, a
leaky refrigerator. We don't even have a
dishwasher.

                    LARRY
You got two hands, don't ya?

                    DORIS
You know what I mean. Now, come on. Have some
stew.

                    LARRY
I'll heat it up when I get home.

                    DORIS
Some appreciation.

                    LARRY
I gotta go.

          SOUND: A DOOR SHUTS.

Scene 2
(Bedroom ambiance)

SOUND: A DOOR SHUTS.

> LARRY

Hon, I'm home.

SOUND: DORIS MUMBLES, HALF ASLEEP.

> LARRY

Did ya hear me?

SOUND: DORIS MUMBLES, HALF ASLEEP.

> LARRY

Come on, wake up. Ya have all day tuh sleep.

SOUND: DORIS MUMBLES, HALF ASLEEP.

> LARRY

Why did ya put the stew away? I said I'd have some when I got home. Hon?

SOUND: DORIS MUMBLES, HALF ASLEEP.

> LARRY

Fine. Keep sleepin'. Lot you care, right? Lot you care.

SOUND: DORIS MUMBLES, HALF ASLEEP.

Scene 3
(Kitchen ambiance)

SOUND: MEAT SIZZLES IN A PAN.

SOUND: A DOOR SHUTS.

                         DORIS

Is that you, Larry?

         SOUND: FOOTSTEPS APPROACH.

                         LARRY

Yes, hon. What's for grub?

                         DORIS

What's it look like?

                         LARRY

Another butcher's special.

                         DORIS

It is, unless you hit the jackpot.

                         LARRY

When are you goin' to do something nice for
me?

                         DORIS

I keep house, don't I? I exercise to stay
trim; I make dinner; all that's for you.
The question is, when are you goin' to do
something for me. It would be nice to go out
on the town once in a while instead of bein'
cooped up in this place all the time . . .
Hey, what's in the box?

                         LARRY

It's for you.

                         DORIS

Really?

                         LARRY

That's what I said.

                         DORIS

You didn't get me a new mop head, did ya?
That was some way to celebrate my thirtieth
birthday.

                         LARRY

I ain't sayin' nothin'.

                    DORIS
Can I open it?

                    LARRY
Sure. Go on.

          SOUND: A CARDBOARD BOX OPENS.

                    DORIS
Would you look at that?!

                    LARRY
So?

                    DORIS
A cuckoo clock! A genuine, cuckoo clock, just
like my ma used to have.

                    LARRY
What do ya think?

                    DORIS
It must have cost a fortune. Is this why you
took that second job? To get this for me?!

                    LARRY
That second job buys my smokes, beer, lottery
tickets.

                    DORIS
And it takes you away from me, going on two
years now.

                    LARRY
I get us by just fine.

                    DORIS
Is that so?!

                    LARRY
Yeah.

                    DORIS
How could you afford this?

                    LARRY
I found it in someone's trash on the way home
from work.

                    DORIS
And here I thought you might actually care
enough to buy me something.

                    LARRY
I care. I pay the bills, don't I?

                    DORIS
But we never go out anymore. We used to have
so much fun.

                    LARRY
You don't have to spend money to have fun.

                    DORIS
Who said anything about spendin' money? We
could take a walk in the park.

                    LARRY
That's for kids and old ladies. Do ya want
the clock or not?

                    DORIS
I want it, but . . .

                    LARRY
What's the matter?

                    DORIS
               (upset)
Nothing. Just leave me alone. I've gotta make
the bed.

        SOUND: A DOOR SLAMS.

                    LARRY
Get out here. I only have a few minutes
before I gotta go to work . . . Come on, hon.
Get out here . . . Do I have to eat alone?
               (MORE)

> LARRY (cont'd)
> . . . All right, I will . . . Uck! Calf's
> liver. The least ya could do is make pasta
> once in a while.[4]

The opening scenes in the scripted example above establish the characters, their socioeconomic status, the dynamic between them, and the main character's story goal. By fleshing out the initial paragraphs of the source material, a full depiction of the characters can be experienced by the audience. Using this technique will enable you to expand short source material into the long form.

Converting Long-Form Source Material into Short Form

Adapting a long-form story, such as a novel, novella, or full-length stage play, into a short audio drama requires attention to the high-level details of the source material. The first step in the process is to outline the major moments in the original story. Next, determine the running time of the adaptation. A ten-minute version would be done differently than a thirty-minute version of the same story. Once the length has been decided upon, review your outline and identify the events that must be dramatized. Depending on the length of the adaptation, certain aspects of the plot may need to be compacted, combined, or cut if they are not deemed crucial to the forward movement of the story.

Let's look at the events that occur in Robert Louis Stevenson's novella *The Strange Case of Dr. Jekyll and Mr. Hyde* and consider how to adapt them into an audio drama. First, we'll list the main story points:

- One night, Gabriel John Utterson and Richard Enfield see a dark figure, Edward Hyde, beat a young woman. They approach Hyde and force him to pay for the woman's injuries.

- Hyde gives Utterson a check signed by Dr. Henry Jekyll. Utterson is concerned that Hyde blackmailed Jekyll to get the check.

- Hyde kills Sir Danvers Carew with a cane.

- Utterson discusses the killing with the police and says he gave Jekyll the cane that was used in the killing.

- Utterson tells Jekyll he is concerned that Hyde forged Jekyll's signature on a note. Jekyll apologizes for causing any trouble. Utterson suspects that Jekyll enabled the note to be created in order to protect Hyde.

- Dr. Hastie Lanyon dies of shock after receiving information relating to Jekyll.

- Jekyll's butler, Mr. Poole, informs Utterson that Jekyll has locked himself in his lab for several weeks now.

- Utterson and Poole break into Jekyll's lab and find Hyde's dead body wearing Jekyll's clothes. A letter from Jekyll is mixed in with the rubble nearby.

- Utterson reads the letter that says Jekyll created a serum that was able to separate a person's good personality traits from their bad. In the process of testing the serum on himself, Jekyll transformed into Hyde. At first, Jekyll was able to use the serum to control the transformations, but eventually they became involuntary and difficult to manage.

- Jekyll's letter reveals that one night Hyde became enraged and killed Carew. Hyde needed help to avoid capture, so he wrote to Lanyon in Jekyll's handwriting, asking his friend to bring chemicals from his lab.

- According to Jekyll's letter, Jekyll then demonstrated to Lanyon how the serum made him transition into Hyde. Lanyon was found dead soon after.

- Jekyll's letter then states that Jekyll's involuntary transformations became more frequent and required more of the serum to undo.
- Later in the letter, Jekyll says that he ran out of an ingredient needed to make the serum. He knew that would lead him to stay transformed as Hyde. Because of that, Jekyll locked himself in his lab, intending to keep Hyde imprisoned.
- Utterson and Poole reflect on the contents of the letter and realize that Jekyll killed his alter ego, Hyde, in the lab, hence killing himself.

After you outline the story, the next step is to determine which plot points are essential for the length of adaptation you are writing. The shorter the adaptation, the less detail that can be included; the longer the version, the more plot and nuances that can be incorporated.

A ten-minute adaptation of *The Strange Case of Dr. Jekyll and Mr. Hyde* may only be able to include up to eight plot points if it takes a page and a half to dramatize each. In this case, Utterson's first encounter with Hyde and his desire to understand the connection between Jekyll and Hyde would need to be established within the first two pages. Pages three to six could focus on a few core clues Utterson uncovers about Jekyll and Hyde. Pages seven through ten would delve into the events that transpire after Utterson finds the letter in Jekyll's lab. When writing a short-form adaptation, consider selecting a few key points to dramatize. That will make the story feel richer and have deeper meaning for the audience.

A thirty-minute audio-drama version of the story can incorporate most of the events in the original story. Each of the main characters' pathos and personalities could be explored as well. Utterson's first encounter with Hyde could unfold within the first five pages of the adaptation. Pages six to fifteen would focus on his encounters with Jekyll and Hyde. Pages twenty through thirty could depict Utterson discovering the letter and learning the truth about Jekyll and Hyde's fate.

After you identify the events you want to include in the adaptation, the next step is to write the script. During the revision process, the page count can be shortened or expanded to meet the desired running time for the adaptation.

Changing the Time Period of a Story

Setting an adaptation in a time period that is different from that of its source material can bring a freshness to the story that creates a whole new audience for the piece. It also gives the writer a great deal of creative freedom. After selecting a story to adapt, identify its universal theme. This is the core meaning of the story that makes it resonate with an audience. Incorporating that meaning into the adaptation will help the script to resonate with listeners.

Next, determine which events in the story will be used to convey the universal theme. Then, delete the aspects of the plot that don't align with this concept. Once you have identified the core events, decide where and when the story is set. There needs to be a compelling reason to change the setting and time period. If you are unsure what that reason is, ask yourself the following questions.

- What prompted you to set the story in the given time period?
- What do you plan to show about life by setting the story in the given time period?
- What benefit do you get from setting the story in the new location and time period?

After you have answered these questions, determine how the events in the original story will be translated into the new setting and time period. Create a biography for each of the main characters that clarifies their background as it pertains to the world found in the adaptation, then decide what length the script will be. When these steps have been completed, you will be ready to create an outline and write the script. To illustrate the process, let's look at a practical example.

William Shakespeare's *Much Ado About Nothing* is a classic, full-length play set in the Elizabethan era. The plot centers around a love triangle between two affluent people: a young maiden, Beatrice, and a soldier, Benedick. Neither recognizes their love for the other. The play's theme, love conquers all, has a universal meaning that transcends time. The adaptation will be thirty minutes long. Limiting the running time enables only the core aspects to be included. Because of this, the B plot that is in the original play will not be included in the audio version.

The story's theme of love can be associated with many things, including the beach and summer. Since that is true, let's set the adaptation in the upscale resort community of Long Beach Island in New Jersey. It will be authentic to the details of the original play, yet modernized. In keeping with that, let's change the character name of Benedick to Ben and Beatrice to Bea. The source material states that Benedick's family originates from Aragon. In the adaptation, Aragon will be the name of the company of which Ben's father is CEO. Bea once worked with Ben at the company and found him to be talented and engaging, yet arrogant. She wants nothing to do with him while on vacation. Her family has unknowingly rented a beach house a few blocks from where his family is staying. She is unhappy when she encounters him and his brother as they arrive for vacation. In the source material, Beatrice and Benedick both wind up at a masquerade ball on a large estate. Let's modernize that to a costume party at the beach house Ben's father is renting. Bea and Ben will talk to each other during the party, though they won't realize who the other is because the costumes they wear mask their true identities. In Shakespeare's play, Beatrice and Benedick's friends do some matchmaking in a garden by setting each of them up so they hear how much the other likes them. Let's set this whispered dialogue in the sand dunes as the main characters walk separately on the beach. The rest of the adaptation will play out similar to the original play in that Bea and Ben confirm their love for one another and plan to get married. Lies are fed to Ben about Bea being with another man. This leads Ben to insult Bea at the altar and break off their relationship. She runs out of the church humiliated. Soon after, Ben realizes that Bea has died and that he was fed lies about her. He confesses his remorse and love for her outside of her house, only to discover that she is still alive. He apologizes. They reunite and have a small, private wedding on the beach.

Notice how the time period, location, and situation have shifted in the scenario above, yet have still remained consistent with the original story. When doing a close to the book adaptation in this category, be sure to revise any humor and dialogue you include from the source material so that it has a modern feel. Taking these steps will enable you to capture the essence of the original story within the adaptation.

Adapting Exposition into Action

Exposition serves an important function in a story. It tells the reader about the characters and their background. Some stories are entirely communicated through the use of exposition, while others are relayed in part through it. Examples include stories written as letters or expressed internally in a character's mind. In audio drama, story events are depicted for the listening audience, not told to them. Translating what is told into what is depicted is an important skill for an audio dramatist to master.

The first step in adapting exposition into active, dramatic storytelling is to determine what pivotal elements are contained within the exposition. Once those aspects have been identified, review them and decide how that information can be depicted in an active way in the script.

Let's look at exposition in Robert Louis Stevenson's novella *The Strange Case of Dr. Jekyll and Mr. Hyde* and discuss how it can be dramatized. The bulk of the novella is told in third person. First-person narrative is used toward the end of the story in a letter that Jekyll wrote. That letter fills in the gaps within the plot. If Utterson is established as the main character, the shift to Jekyll's first-person exposition presents a challenge when adapting the novella. In order for Utterson to continue to be seen as the protagonist, he needs to be active while the information in Jekyll's letter is revealed. Utterson's goal in the story is to understand what became of Jekyll. One way to use Jekyll's expository letter in an active way is to have Utterson read excerpts to Jekyll's servant, Poole. This can be combined with flashbacks of events mentioned in the letter and Utterson trying to make sense of it all. Blending these three techniques will create tense active storytelling and enable Utterson to solve the mystery in the process.

A second method that can be used to dramatize the exposition in Dr. Jekyll's letter is to make Jekyll the protagonist. In this case, the events in his letter will become the main story. The third-person narrative and other pivotal expository elements should be interspersed throughout Jekyll's journey to flesh out the story in an active manner while Jekyll attempts to separate the good and bad from his personality, which leads to a tragic outcome.

The two approaches discussed above are effective ways to dramatize expository information. If the source material you adapt contains large amounts of exposition, determine what the most effective way to reveal those elements through action is. Doing so will enable you to create an engaging in-the-moment adaptation.

Adapting Visually Driven Source Material into Audio Drama

Adapting visual moments from a novel, short story, or screenplay into the audio-drama format requires focus on the aural details of the situation being dramatized. Using this approach will enable the listener to visualize the events in their mind. Action elements, such as fights and chases, should be depicted step by step so that each component is fully illustrated through sound cues and dialogue. This requires a clear setup, followed by a blend of sound effects and dialogue, to communicate each action as it unfolds.

Let's look at an example from the beginning of Jules Verne's novel *Mysterious Island*. The text states:

> *The cords which attached the basket to the hoop were cut, and the balloon, as the former fell into the sea, rose again 2,000 feet. This was, indeed, the last means of lightening the apparatus. The five passengers had clambered into the net around the hoop, and, clinging to its meshes, looked into the abyss below.*
>
> *Everyone knows the statical sensibility of a balloon. It is only necessary to relieve it of the lightest object in order to have it rise. The apparatus floating in air acts like a mathematical balance. One can readily understand, then, that when disencumbered of every weight relatively great, its upward movement will be sudden and considerable. It was thus in the present instance. But after remaining poised for a moment at its height, the balloon began to descend. It was impossible to repair the rent, through which the gas was rushing, and the men having done everything they could do, must look to God for succor.[5]*

This passage puts the reader in the middle of a tense moment. Plot is communicated through action and exposition that is not associated with a specific character. To adapt an active moment like this into an audio play, first clarify what is happening, then associate each action with a specific character. That character will be responsible for communicating the action, as is demonstrated in the audio version of the section of *Mysterious Island* that follows.

                    PENCROFF
    Herbert, help me cut the suspension cords.

                    HERBERT
    Yes, sir.

        SOUND: ROPE BEING CUT.

                    CYRUS
    Why are you doing that?!

                    PENCROFF
    To get rid of the basket.

                    SPILETT
    Are you out of your mind?!

                    PENCROFF
    We have to lose the weight or we'll die.

                    CYRUS
    There must be another way!

                    HERBERT
    We're down to the last two cords, Father.

                    PENCROFF
    Let's cut them.

        SOUND: ROPE BEING CUT.

                    PENCROFF
    Everybody, grab onto the net below the
    balloon.

                    HERBERT
    Come here, Top!

        SOUND: A DOG BARKS.

                              HERBERT
Good boy!

                              SPILETT
It's never going to hold us.

                              PENCROFF
Grab on now or it will be too late!

        SOUND: FRANTIC CLIMBING INTO A NET AS A
        BASKET FALLS AWAY AND INTO THE OCEAN.

                              CYRUS
We made it!

                              SPILETT
We're still descending.

                              NEB
Not as quickly, though.
                        (beat)
Oh, no! We're going in!

        SOUND: THE NET PLUNGES INTO THE OCEAN.

        MUSIC: ASCENDS.

                              SPILETT
                        (waterlogged)
Hang on! Don't let go!

        SOUND: THE WIND BLOWS.[6]

Adapting visual source material such as this into audio drama requires
a balance of sound effects and dialogue. The dialogue needs to be brief and
authentic to the situation. Sound effects should clarify the actions that occur.
Using each of these tools precisely will enable you to craft a powerful, action-
filled audio adaptation.

Adapting a Story from One Genre to Another

Switching genres is an innovative approach to consider when adapting a story into an audio play. Imagine changing the adventure story *Swiss Family Robinson* into a farce, *Rumpelstiltskin* into a romance, or *20,000 Leagues Under the Sea* into a horror story. These may sound like unusual ideas, but if you find the right way into the adaptation, it could reimagine the story in an exciting new way.

Let's look at the steps needed to adapt a story from one genre to another. First, choose a story that intrigues you. Next, determine what underlying themes in the story you want to explore by changing the genre. Once that has been decided, select the genre that will enable you to achieve your goal. After that, outline the major plot points in the story. Review the outline and determine what aspects will be altered and in what ways. Consider how the characters will change and react to story events in the new genre. Finally, make sure each plot point encompasses the feel of the new genre. When that is done, you are ready to write the script.

In order to better understand how this type of adaptation works, let's look at a practical example. We'll convert the adventure story *Swiss Family Robinson* into a farce. Below is an outline of the main events that occur in the novel.

- One night at sea, a ship encounters a turbulent storm. The Robinson family, comprised of William; his wife, Elizabeth; and their four sons, Fritz, Ernest, Jack, and Franz, are left to battle the storm alone after the rest of the passengers depart in the ship's only lifeboat.
- The Robinsons awake the next morning in calm water and spot an island in the distance.
- The family finds a makeshift vessel onboard the ship. They fill it with food and head for the island.

- They reach shore and set up camp.
- William and his oldest son, Fritz, search the island for a permanent place to live.
- The family runs out of food and travels back to the ship to get more.
- They construct a treehouse in which to live.
- Each son builds their own home to have a private space.
- The family erects a farmhouse.
- They set up a house in a cave.
- Fritz discovers a young Englishwoman, Jenny, who was shipwrecked on the other side of the island.
- A British ship comes to rescue the Robinsons and Jenny.
- Jenny and two Robinson sons head back to civilization on the ship, but most of the family decide to remain on the island and live their life out together in solitude.

In the genre of farce, characters are typically one-dimensional. They serve a specific purpose, but the audience doesn't care about them. This makes outlandish plots more plausible for an audience to accept. Even though characters are less developed in this genre, each needs to be distinct. Let's define the characters as they will appear in the adaptation.

William – Egotistical, values his ambitious and illogical son, Ernest, over his more logical son, Fritz.

Elizabeth – Smart, but goes along with her husband's poor decisions, thinking he'll learn from his mistakes someday. However, he never does.

Fritz – A walking, teenage hormone.

Ernest – A whiny tagalong who is awful when it comes to logic and usually wrong about everything he says.

Jack – A sadistic pest.

Franz – A complainer, a real pain in the behind.

Jenny – Charming, of sound mind and body.

The theme of the original story is family unity. The adaptation will use this theme as well, emphasizing that family members have shared experiences that bond them together for good and bad. The eldest son, Fritz, will be the protagonist. Now that these main elements are in place, let's use them to outline the plot of the adaptation.

- A ship, the S.S. *Shtinkenhauser*, is tossed during a life-threatening storm at sea. The crew attempts to help the Robinson family escape onto a lifeboat. The family's squabbling exasperates the crew. They are forced to leave the family behind in order to save the rest of the passengers and themselves. The family is so consumed with their bickering that they don't realize they have been abandoned.
- When the Robinsons' quarreling subsides, Fritz encourages the family to seek shelter inside the ship. William takes Ernest's suggestion and demands they remain on deck until a rescue ship arrives. The family is drenched and tossed back and forth all night, barely able to hang on to the ship.
- The next morning, the Robinsons awaken. Several family members have colds. Fritz spots an island in the near distance and points it out. Ernest is quick to take credit for Fritz's discovery as Franz complains

ad nauseum about not feeling well. William shoos him away and proclaims that their experience on deck the night before was invigorating. Franz keels over and dies. William is glad to have the silence and says with Franz gone there's one less mouth to feed. Fritz encourages the family to forge onward to the island, where salvation awaits and hopefully some pretty girls his age as well.

- Fritz encourages the family to get in a tub and row over to the island. They argue incessantly about who will be the first passenger to get in the tub. In the process, they cause the tub to sink, which leaves them with no choice but to swim to the island on random pieces of wood they find floating in the ocean.

- Fritz helps his father set up a camp on the beach as Jack finds a crab in the surf and chases his brothers with it, causing the crab to pinch them.

- William heads off to find a permanent place for the family to live on the island. Fritz begs to come along in the hope of finding some girls. William agrees. Ernest tags behind. When they encounter a natural crossroad, Fritz suggests they go in one direction. Ernest is positive they can make it through a shorter section, even though it is replete with quicksand traps. They walk into the quicksand and are barely able to help one another escape alive. Afterward, Ernest shrugs off his mistake. William pats him on the head for trying while Fritz fumes.

- Back at camp, Jack gets pinched by the crabs as Elizabeth looks on with subtle joy. William, Fritz, and Ernest return and say they have found the perfect spot to build a home.

- The Robinsons construct a treehouse in the woods. Fritz and his father work well together. Meanwhile, Jack goes around hitting everyone in the leg with a board and Ernest nails Jack's pants to a tree to stop him from being a nuisance, then brags incessantly about how great he is. Fritz has his fill of Ernest's gloating and shoves a beehive over his head to shut him up. Elizabeth shrugs her sons' behavior off as she tends their injuries.

- Soon after, Fritz tires of the family's constant bickering. He heads off and builds a home of his own. Whiny copycats Ernest and Jack nag their parents, who help them build their own homes in an attempt to have privacy and peace as well.

- Fritz enjoys the time alone in his home, yet longs for female companionship.

- Food begins to run low for all.

- Ernest and Jack become lonely and hungry while living on their own. Even Fritz misses the family connection, however dysfunctional it may be.

- The family decides to come together to build a farmhouse, where they plan to grow food for one and all.

- Fritz insists on growing lettuce; however, his brothers want to plant other vegetables. Each grabs the seeds they want to grow. An argument ensues among them, leading all of the seeds to fall to the ground in a mess.

- Before long, a menagerie of vegetables grows entangled together on the land. They strangle each other and die, leaving the family with no food.

- Fritz has had enough of the family and sets out to find food in the woods. In the process, he encounters a young woman named Jenny who recently became stranded on the island. There is an instant attraction between them. Fritz wants them to live together alone in the woods. However, Jenny insists they return to Fritz's home so she can meet his family.

- Fritz introduces Jenny to the family. Each son has an eye for her. She declines. They bicker and prod Jenny until she is ready to pull her hair out.
- Ernest and Jack playfully chase Jenny up a palm tree and then encourage her to come down. She refuses. She's had enough of their craziness.
- Fritz tries to entice Jenny to head off with him. She won't.
- Ernest and Jack chop the palm tree down in an effort to reach Jenny. As they do, Jenny spots a ship approaching in the distance.
- The tree falls into the sea with Jenny on it. Fritz watches, worried he'll lose her.
- Jenny swims out to the ship and tells the crew that the family on the island is insane. The ship takes Jenny off to safety, leaving the family stuck on the island.
- Fritz can't believe that the family's squabbling hurt his chance to have female companionship and hurt the family's chance to get off the island. He realizes that even if the family had been rescued, he'd still be stuck with them, so the island is as good a place as any to live out the rest of their lives together. Elizabeth nods with a smile as their bickering starts again. Fritz realizes that family dynamics are tough to navigate, but at least they have a bond.

The process illustrated above demonstrates the effect switching from one genre to another can have on a story when it is adapted. All forms of adaptation create the opportunity to bring stories to new audiences. Through solid technique and innovation, an audio dramatist can transform a story into an audio play that will engage listeners in unique and exciting ways.

Chapter 10
Series

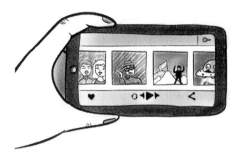

Writing for an audio-drama series can provide consistent work for a writer. Unlike television, where a large staff of writers develops a series together in a "writers' room," audio-drama series are generally driven by a production head and one or two writers. Working on a series gives you a great deal of creative freedom as an audio dramatist. There are two paths that can lead to work on a show. The first involves identifying an existing program you want to write for and then reaching out to the producers; the second is to create your own series and pitch it to an audio-drama company.

If you are interested in writing for an existing show, you will need to have written some audio-drama scripts in a comparable style to the series for which you are looking to write. If you don't have any, take time to write some. Once you have, you will be ready to reach out to producers. See chapter 17 for guidance on the submission process.

When you create your own audio-drama series, you will need to write a proposal, which consists of a series bible and the script for the first episode. The steps needed to craft each of these is detailed below. Regardless of whether you create a new series or strive to work on an existing one, it is important to understand how a show is constructed. This chapter will provide you with the information you need to know. Let's get started.

Series Types

There are several kinds of audio-drama series. Each has its own rules and falls into one of the categories below:

> Anthology series. Each episode is a complete story that is set in a unique world and features characters that won't appear again in the series.
>
> Miniseries. A story that unfolds over a limited number of episodes. When the storyline ends, the series is over.
>
> Soap opera. A program that uses the epic structure and features stories that are depicted over a number of episodes. When one storyline ends, another begins.
>
> Stand-alone episode series. Each episode is a complete story that centers around specific, recurring characters who are involved in an ongoing situation.

Sources to Find Series Ideas

The success of an audio-drama series depends upon the strength of its concept and its characters. A series needs to have an engaging premise in order to generate continual story ideas. The characters should be distinct and relatable to the audience. Ideas for series can come from many different sources.

Short stories are an ideal source of material from which to craft an audio series. Their compact nature makes it easy to define the story's world, characters, and basic situation. Short stories that are part of a series can help generate material for additional episodes of a program.

Novels contain an in-depth look at characters and their situation, which makes them a rich source from which to adapt a series. They can be used in a couple of ways. One method is to take a specific number of chapters and adapt them into a single episode. For example, chapters 1 to 5 of a book could be adapted into the first episode of a series, and chapters 6 to 10 could be adapted into the second episode. This works well for novels that have sequels or are serialized. Another option is to base a series exclusively on a book's premise and characters. In this case, episodes do not need to be directly derived from the plot of the book.

Consider using a story you wrote in another medium as source material for a series. This approach has the potential to open up your work to a new audience. Refer to chapter 9 for adaptation techniques that can help you create a series based upon material in this category.

You can map off of an existing story to create a series. To do so, select a story that resonates with an audience and populate its high-level structure with an original concept and unique characters. If you base your series on popular source material, it will have a strong likelihood of being successful. See chapter 8 for complete details on the mapping process.

Create a series based upon an original concept. Infuse your idea with distinct characters, situations, and ways of tackling obstacles. Be sure to acquaint yourself with series in the same genre. If you find that your show is similar to one that exists, evolve your idea into something that has not been done before.

How to Develop a Story Idea into a Series

Every story begins as an idea. When you select a concept to develop into a series, be sure it is relatable to an audience, contains a situation that is rich with dramatic potential, and has characters that are full of idiosyncrasies. If the concept is based upon a novel, feature the most dynamic characters from the novel in the series. If you map a series concept off of an existing story, construct characters that are in line with the qualities found in the high-level structure of the source material from which you are mapping.

Once you have chosen an idea on which to base your series, identify the main dramatic conflict. For concepts derived from source material, this information can be found within the original story. If you are developing an original idea, determine what universal aspect is at the heart of the idea and flesh it out. Next, define the type of show you are creating. It could be an anthology, miniseries, soap opera, or stand-alone episode series. After that, decide how long each episode is and the number of episodes that will comprise a season. While these aspects are entirely up to you, many series are comprised of six to twelve thirty-minute episodes per season.

Now that you have established the core qualities of the series, you are ready to brainstorm storylines. Start by reviewing the main characters and their primary conflict. Write down potential situations that could arise as a result of the conflict and the dynamic between the characters. If you are using existing source material, select situations from it that complement the concept you have chosen for the series. Write down as many story ideas as you can think of, then create a short list that features the strongest. Flesh out each short-listed idea into a one-paragraph summary until you have enough storylines for a full season of episodes.

For series that contain a B plot, the next step is to determine what the high-level view of that storyline will be for the season. B plots usually focus on the main character's private life or aspects of the story world that are not explored in the A plot. When developing a B plot, consider how the main character will evolve during the season. Ask yourself what the audience understands about the character at the start of the season and how that will change by the end of the season. You can add twists and even end the season's

B plot with a cliffhanger enticing listeners to return next season to find out what happens. If your series contains supporting characters, consider fleshing out their lives in the B plot as well.

C plots are optional and if included do not occur as frequently as B plots do. They provide a tertiary layer of storytelling within a given season. Start by deciding what your intent is for the C plot. Ask yourself whether it will culminate as the focus of the last few episodes of the season or solely give the series greater depth. Once this has been determined, plot out each occurrence of the C plot, noting in which episodes it will occur and how it will affect the season overall.

Let's look at a practical example of how to develop an audio-drama series. The early twentieth-century dime novel serial *The Liberty Boys of '76* will be used as source material. *The Liberty Boys of '76* is set during the American Revolutionary War. It centers around a teenage character, Dick Slater, and his efforts to help General Washington win the war. Each issue of the dime novel serial is a blend of fact and fiction. The aspects that revolve around the war are true, while the character of Dick and his family are fictional. The A plot immerses the protagonist, whom we will modernize to call Dan Slater for the show, in a series of missions to help General Washington gain information that will aid him in winning the war.

The dime novel's B plot revolves around Dick's home life. He and his friend, Bob Estabrooke, return home to their families whenever possible. In each issue of the dime novel serial, the family is glad to see them and worries about them when they leave. While this is an authentic reaction for a soldier's family to have, it is uneventful as a B plot. To make it engaging in the audio-drama series, we'll have Dan's girlfriend, Alice, be civic-minded. She'll attempt to bring people with opposing views about the war together at social gatherings to help them see they have more in common than their differences. Giving Alice this quality turns her into an active character with an objective and obstacles to overcome. It also endears her to Dan, who believes in her cause.

Each issue of *The Liberty Boys of '76* series ends with a compact, yet fast-paced battle that features Dick and his troops aiding General Washington's men in the war. While these moments are exciting, the fact that they take multiple steps to unfold makes them complicated to adapt in the series format. The most effective way to do so is to focus on the aspects that move the plot forward in a concise and easy to follow manner.

The A and B plots in the example above work hand in hand to create an active story with engaging, complex characters. The A plot is the main focus of each episode, while the B plot gives the audience insight into who the main character and his family are. Once you have defined the plot layers in your series, you are ready for the next step, writing a series bible.

The Series Bible

A series bible details the inner workings of an audio-drama series, everything from the story rules to episode summaries. There are two types of bibles: the first establishes the groundwork for a proposed new series, the second is used to keep an existing series consistent during production.

Bibles for proposed new series help the writer document and develop the show. They are also used to promote the show to producers. This type of bible should be written in the tone of the show. If you are developing a comedy, use humor in the narrative style of the bible. If you are creating a thriller, incorporate an air of suspense.

Series bibles that are written for existing audio-drama programs help the production team track the characters, plots, story world, and other details necessary to ensure that the show is consistent and does not become repetitive. This type of bible is for internal use of the production only. The main writer updates it on an ongoing basis and includes as much information as needed to describe the evolution of the show. The bible is also given to writers who join the staff during the program's run so they can quickly become acquainted with the nuances of writing for the series.

A series bible contains the core elements of a series, each of which is discussed below. When writing a bible, be sure to include all required aspects. Doing so will help you to flesh out the series and present the information in a professional way.

The basic format of a series bible includes the use of an easy to read, twelve-point font, such as Arial. The text is single spaced. Margins are one inch on all sides. All pages are numbered except for the title page.

Title Page

This element is laid out similarly to the title page of a script. One-fourth from the top and centered, include the title of the series in capital letters. Skip one line, center the text, write the word "by" and then [insert the series bible writer's name]. If the series is based upon source material, skip two lines, center the text, and write "Based on the [Insert the word novel/short story/etc.] [Insert the title of the source material in quotes] by [Insert the source material writer's name]." If the source material line is extensive, break it up onto more than one line. Bibles used to promote a new series should include the writer's contact information flush left at the bottom of the page. The writer's name and email address are required. Phone number and mailing address are optional. Contact information is not included on production bibles. Instead enter the date of the latest version of the bible such as "10/12/2022" for the initial draft and "Rev. 1/4/2023" for subsequent drafts.

Premise

Describe the overall concept of the series in one to two sentences. This is a high-level look at the show. Refer to characters in descriptive terms, not by proper names. This is done to enrich and clarify the premise. For example, you could say, "Ray takes a job fighting forest fires." However, the reader will not know who Ray is. If you write, "An aging, diabetic fireman takes a job fighting forest fires," the reader will have a clear sense of who the main character is and the general concept of the story.

Synopsis

This section features a one-paragraph summary of the series concept. Character names may be used as long as they are followed by a brief description. For example, "Ray, an aging, diabetic fireman, takes a job fighting forest fires in California." This description expands upon the information that was provided about the character in the "premise" section. Additional details about the show's plot are included in this section of the bible as well.

Story World

Detail what makes the world in your series unique, including specific social rules, attitudes, and customs. This section is optional for a proposed new series but highly recommended for shows that are in production because it tracks the evolution of the show's world. It is updated as needed to capture changes.

Main Characters

List the main characters in order of their prominence within the series, starting with the protagonist. Each character's name is followed by a space, a dash, and then another space. Next, describe the character, including their age and personality traits. Keep the description brief, anywhere from one sentence to one paragraph.

Main Story Locations

List the locations in which the series takes place and a brief description of each. Include both a physical and aural description. This section is optional for a new series and recommended for existing ones. For a new series, it highlights the main settings for potential producers. For existing series, it helps the production team track the primary locations and the sound effects used to create them.

Episode Log

If you are proposing a new series, an episode log is required. Each entry in the log begins with a label that is underlined and starts with the word "episode" in capital letters. That is followed by a space, the episode number, another space, an en dash, a space, and the episode title, which is in quotes. An example follows.

EPISODE 1 – "Fighting for Freedom"

Include a one-paragraph summary for each of the first six episodes. Use character names instead of descriptions of characters and discuss the A, B, and C plots when applicable.

An episode log is optional for series in production. When it is included, consider writing a one-sentence synopsis for each episode. Doing so will document the storyline and help you avoid using similar themes in future episodes.

A sample series bible for a proposed new show appears on the following pages. It is included here for use as a guide.

.

THE LIBERTY BOYS
By John Smith

Based upon the dime novel series
"The Liberty Boys of '76" by Harry Moore

John Smith
35 Blake St., Apt 43
Lipton, AZ 89899
(623) 390-3039
John.Smith@gmail.com

The Liberty Boys

Premise
A young man becomes a militia leader and spy in order to help the United States secure independence from Great Britain during the Revolutionary War.

Synopsis
After a difference of opinion about the Revolutionary War kills diplomat Roger Slater, his teenage son, Dan, takes up his cause by forming a militia group and assisting General Washington in his pursuit to free the United States from British rule. Meanwhile, Dan's girlfriend, Alice, and his sister, Edith, organize community events back home to help people realize that they have more in common than different.

Story World
The series is set in 1776 in Tarrytown, New York, and various parts of the region, just after the Declaration of Independence is signed. It uses a fictive character, Dan Slater, and his militia group, the Liberty Boys, to bring the history of the American Revolutionary War to life through a series of tense, undercover missions and battles.

Main Characters
Dan Slater – A seventeen-year-old, courageous militia leader and spy for General Washington, believes the United States will be stronger if it is independent from Great Britain's rule.

Bob Estabrooke – A seventeen-year-old, daring close friend of Dan's, leads the militia group when Dan is on a mission for General Washington and occasionally partners with him on missions when needed.

Alice Estabrooke – Sixteen years old, Bob's sister and Dan's girlfriend, caring, civic-minded, leads community initiatives aimed at bringing people in Tarrytown, New York, together to help them move past their differences and value what they have in common.

Edith Slater – Sixteen years old, Dan's sister and Bob's girlfriend, enterprising, independent, assists Alice in her initiative to bring the people of Tarrytown, New York, together.

General Washington – Mid-forties, bold, principled general of the Continental Army.

Episode Log

EPISODE 1 – "Fighting for Freedom"

After Dan Slater's father is killed by neighbors for expressing his support of the United States' independence from Great Britain, Dan forms a militia group of his peers and leads them to General Washington's post to affirm support for his mission. The general is impressed with Dan's abilities and enlists his help to get information that will aid the United States in winning the war.

EPISODE 2 – "Settling with the British and Tories"

Dan sneaks into British military headquarters and learns that the Redcoats plan to attack the United States at Throgg's Neck. He relays this information to General Washington, which helps the United States win a battle. Afterward, Dan returns home, proud to learn that his girlfriend, Alice, is organizing a social event in the hope of bridging the differences between people in town.

EPISODE 3 – "Helping General Washington"

General Washington enlists Dan's help to uncover the Redcoats' next move. A resident of a nearby town gives Dan shelter when he is almost caught. He reveals he was close with British intelligence but recently turned Patriot. He gives Dan insight into the Brit's war plans. Dan makes his way back to General Washington's fort with the information and helps ward off a surprise attack by the Redcoats.

EPISODE 4 – "Always in the Right Place"

When bullies get rough in Tarrytown, Dan and Bob defend their girlfriends' right to help people. Shortly after, they return to Washington's post and find it besieged by Redcoats. Dan and the Liberty Boys help the general's troops fend them off.

EPISODE 5 – "Not Afraid of the King's Minions"

General Washington asks Dan to deliver a message to General Greene at Fort Washington. Dan arrives to find Redcoats storming the fort. He and the Liberty Boys fight the British, only to be overpowered. Dan and his troops retreat to Fort Lee, where Dan informs the general that the

Redcoats have captured Fort Washington. They hurry inside as the Brits start to fire at them.

EPISODE 6 – "Catch and Hang Us If You Can"
General Washington sends Dan and Bob to ask General Lee for aid in battling the British. Dan and Bob return with news that Lee is unable to assist. As the Redcoats close in, Washington orders the fort evacuated. All flee into the nearby woods.

Once the series bible has been completed, the next step is to write the script for the pilot episode. After that, you will be ready to submit your show to audio-drama companies for their consideration. For information on how to write a script, see chapter 9.

Chapter 11
Script Formatting

Audio drama is a collaborative form of storytelling. Proper script formatting contributes to that process by enabling actors to easily locate their lines, editors to identify sound notations, and composers to spot music cues. When working for an audio-drama production company, format scripts to their specifications; otherwise, use the general audio-drama script format, which is detailed below.

Every audio-drama script includes three basic components: a title page, a character page, and the text of the script. All pages should be typed in Courier 12-point font. The top, bottom, and right margins are set at 1 inch. The left margin is set at 1.5 inches.

Title Page

The title page provides essential information about a script and includes the following components.

> Title. This element is the name of the script. It is centered, one-fourth down from the top of the page, in capital letters. For a series, enter

the series title, followed by the season number, a period, the episode number, a colon, and then the title of the episode such as:

```
ON THE VERGE 1.1: THE DILEMMA
```

Byline. This component identifies who wrote the script. It is centered directly below the title and contains the word "by" followed by the audio dramatist's name. It is written as follows.

```
By John Smith
```

Source Material Line. This section references the material upon which a script was based. It is used when a script is an adaptation. The source material line is positioned two lines under the byline. The text is centered and contains the following verbiage: "Based on the [Insert the word novel/short story/etc.] [Insert the story title in quotes] by [Insert the source material writer's name]." An example appears below.

```
Based on the novel
"Wuthering Heights" by Emily Brontë
```

Contact Information. This area features the audio dramatist's name and email address. Mailing address and phone number are optional. It appears at the bottom left corner of the title page. An example follows:

```
John Smith
35 Blake St., Apt 43
Lipton, AZ 89899
(623) 390-3039
John.Smith@gmail.com
```

<u>Draft Information.</u> This section details the script's revision history. If a script is written for or acquired by a company, draft information replaces the audio dramatist's contact information at the bottom left corner of the title page. Companies consider the draft they acquire from an audio dramatist to be the first draft. Subsequent drafts are numbered sequentially. Version information is written in capital letters and includes the word "draft," the draft number, and the draft completion date, which is enclosed in parentheticals. Each time a version of the script is completed, the new draft information is written in bold above the previous information as follows:

DRAFT 3 (5/6/2023)
DRAFT 2 (5/4/2023)
DRAFT 1 (12/6/2022)

A sample title page for an audio-drama series appears on the next page. It is included here for use as a guide.

ON THE VERGE 1.1: THE DILEMMA

By John Smith

John Smith

35 Blake St., Apt 43

Lipton, AZ 89899

(623) 390-3039

John.Smith@gmail.com

Character Page

The character page provides a basic description of each character that appears in the script. It is placed directly after the title page. The character page consists of the following components.

> Page Label. This element establishes that the page contains information about the characters found in the script. The word "characters" is centered at the top of the page in capital letters. The word "alphabetical" is centered on the line below in parentheticals and is written in lower-case letters. The term within the parentheticals signifies that the character list that follows appears in alphabetical order.

> Character List. This section contains information about each character who appears in the script. After the page label component, skip one line and enter information for the first character on the list. Each entry begins with the character name in capital letters, followed by a space, an en dash, and then another space. That is followed, in sentence case, by a brief description of the character's age and personal attributes. Each entry is separated by one line. The character list assists producers with casting and gives the actors insight into the roles they are playing. An example follows.

```
JACK'S MOTHER — Mid-forties, caring, office
worker, loves her son and husband very much.
```

> Time/Setting. This line states the era and location in which the story takes place. After the last entry in the character list, skip two lines and type the words "time/setting" in capital letters, a colon, and then a brief description of the time and setting of the story such as:

```
Present day. Mansfield, Pennsylvania.
```

Author's Note. This section is included if an aspect of the script needs to be clarified. Below time/setting, skip one line. In brackets, type the phrase "author's note" in title case followed by a colon. Insert the text of the note in sentence case as in the example below.

```
[Author's Note: Bracketed dialogue should be
said in Spanish. An English translation is
provided for reading purposes only.]
```

The following character page is from episode 1.1 of *On the Verge*. It is included here for use as a guide.

CHARACTERS
(alphabetical)

EMMA — Twenty years old, fun-loving college student.

FEMALE CUSTOMER — Early thirties, well-off jewelry store patron.

INMATE #1 — Early twenties, charming, manipulator.

INMATE #2 — Early twenties, gruff, schemer.

JACK BRAYDEN — Twenty years old, college student and jewelry store clerk.

JACK'S BOSS — Mid-fifties, patient, supportive, owner of a jewelry store.

JACK'S MOTHER — Mid-forties, caring, office worker, loves her son and husband very much.

JACK'S STEPFATHER — Mid-forties, take-charge manager at an electronics corporation, compassionate yet competitive for Jack's mother's affection.

JAIL GUARD — Late thirties, stern overseer, doesn't take lip from anyone.

JUDGE — Mid-fifties, no-nonsense jurist who occasionally cracks a smile.

MR. WOLAWSKI — Mid-forties, high school P.E. teacher, enjoys mentoring his students.

POLICE OFFICER — Late thirties, friendly, takes his job seriously and does everything by the book.

PUBLIC DEFENSE ATTORNEY — Forty-five years old, skilled, stressed, and overworked lawyer.

STEW — Twenty years old, college student, daredevil, can be jealous and bullish at times.

TIME/SETTING: Present Day. Mansfield, Pennsylvania.

[Author's Note: Bracketed dialogue should be said in Spanish. An English translation is provided for reading purposes only.]

Script

The general audio-drama script format is laid out so that each page equals one minute of running time. It consists of the following components.

> Page Number. All pages except for the first page are numbered. Numbers should be placed flush right at the top of the page, followed by a period and a blank line.
>
> Scene Header. This element identifies the start of a scene. It is used for reference purposes during the production. The scene header is centered and underlined. It is comprised of the word "scene," which is written in sentence case, followed by a space and then a sequential number, as in the example below.

<u>Scene 1</u>

Ambient Sound Line. This component is used to communicate the ambient noises that are heard during a scene. It appears directly below the scene header, is centered, and is written in sentence case between parentheticals as in the following example.

(City street ambiance)

Sound Effect Line. This element is used to describe noises that are essential to tell the story. It is positioned at the second tab from the left margin, underlined, and written in capital letters. The sound effect line begins with the identifying tag "sound." It is followed by a colon and a short description of a sound. If multiple noises are heard, each should be written on a separate line. If a specific character cries, sneezes, screams, etc., include this information on the sound effect line. Examples of key uses of this element are below.

Multiple sounds:

<u>SOUND: A CAR ENGINE TURNS OFF.</u>

<u>SOUND: A CAR DOOR OPENS.</u>

<u>SOUND: FEET STEP ONTO PAVEMENT.</u>

<u>SOUND: A CAR DOOR SHUTS.</u>

Character sounds:

<u>A. SOUND: JACK SNEEZES.</u>

<u>B. SOUND: MR. WOLAWSKI SNAPS HIS FINGERS.</u>

C. SOUND: JACK'S STEPFATHER GRUNTS.

Music Line. This element describes the various types of music that are used in a script. These include musical scoring, music heard on a radio or TV, music used to transition from one scene to another, and music that enhances a specific moment in a scene. The music line is positioned at the second tab from the left margin. It is underlined and written in capital letters. This component starts with the identifying tag "music." It is followed by a colon and then a short description of the music that is heard. An initial line signifies when the music starts, a second line notes when it ends. An example follows.

MUSIC: A TRANQUIL MELODY FADES UP.

                    JACK'S MOTHER
Sleep well.
                         JACK
Thanks, Mom.

MUSIC: THE TRANQUIL MELODY FADES OUT.

Character Header. This element identifies the name of the character who says the dialogue directly below it. It is center tabbed and written in capital letters. As a rule, each character should be referred to by one consistent name in the character header, even if that character is revealed to have a different name in the dialogue at some point. This is done so that everyone associated with the production has a clear understanding of which lines go with which characters. If a character's dialogue is broken up by a sound effect or music line, the continuation of that dialogue is noted in the character header by writing "(cont'd)" after the character's name in the following manner:

                              STEW
    That's what happened as far as I remember
    . . . Yup--

        SOUND: A CELL PHONE DROPS ON THE FLOOR.

        SOUND: RUSTLING AS A CELL PHONE IS
        PICKED UP.

                              STEW (cont'd)
    Sorry about that. I dropped my phone. Where
    were we?

Character Parenthetical. This line provides clarity regarding the dialogue
    that follows it. It is comprised of a brief description, written between
    two parentheticals in lower-case letters. The character parenthetical
    appears directly below the character header and is located four tabs
    in from the left margin. It has four uses. The first is to clarify tone. If
    a character says something in a sarcastic manner, a parenthetical may
    be used to clarify the intent of the line such as:

                        JACK
                   (sarcastic)
    I'm sure you care a lot.

The second use signifies to whom a character is speaking. It is used when a
character switches from addressing one character to another during a single
line of dialogue. For example . . .

                        JACK
    Yes, sir. I understand.
                   (to Female Customer)
    I'm sorry, ma'am. We don't have that in
    stock.

The third use notes a brief pause within a single line of dialogue, as in the following:

```
                    POLICE OFFICER
        License and registration.

            SOUND: PAPERS SHUFFLE.

                    POLICE OFFICER (cont'd)
        Thank you.
                (beat)
        Brayden. I gave you a warning for running a
        yellow light a few months ago.
```

In the example above, the beat represents the moment that the police officer reviews the license and registration. The fourth use identifies the need for a technical effect, such as when a character is heard speaking on the other end of the phone, on the radio, or on TV, as in the following example.

```
                    EMMA
            (on car phone speaker)
        Don't be long or the party will start without
        you.
```

Dialogue. This element consists of the words that a character says. It is the main component in an audio-drama script. Since that is the case, dialogue is given more space on the page than the other elements. In terms of formatting, character speech begins at the left margin and ends at the right margin.

Simultaneous Dialogue. This component is defined as two characters speaking at the same time. It is not used frequently. When it is, both character headers appear on the same line. The first character header is one tab in from the left margin and the second character header is one tab in from the right margin. Character parentheticals are three spaces in from their respective margin. Dialogue for character one is flush with the left margin and ends fifteen spaces after the character header. Dialogue for character two begins five spaces before the second character header and ends flush with the right margin, as follows:

```
        JACK                          STEW
      (surprised)                   (laughs)
  I don't know what            Don't play dumb
  you're talking about?        with me.
```

End-of-Page Requirements. This element defines how each page in a script ends. A page should conclude at the end of a sentence. This is done so that actors don't need to turn the page in the middle of a sentence. Neither a character header nor a parenthetical may end a page. They must be followed by dialogue. If you find that a page ends with either a character header or a parenthetical, move the elements to the top of the next page. At the bottom of the initial page, type the word "more" in capital letters between two parentheticals four tabs in from the left margin. The character header at the top of the next page should be followed by "(cont'd)." This is done so the actor playing the role understands that their speech continues on the next page such as:

```
                    JACK
  After that, I came back here.
                  (MORE)
```

```
                                            18.
```

```
                    JACK (cont'd)
  I don't remember what time it was, though.
```

The following scene from episode 1.1 of *On the Verge* is included here for use as a script formatting guide.

4.

Scene 2
(Interior car ambiance)

MUSIC: A HEAVY-METAL INSTRUMENTAL PLAYS IN THE BACKGROUND.

SOUND: A CAR'S TURN SIGNAL CLICKS.

JACK
I'm on my way, Emma.

EMMA
(on car phone speaker)
Don't be long or the party will start without you.

JACK
My birthday party?!

EMMA
That's right. We'll eat all the cake before you get here so you won't be able to blow out the candles.

JACK
Hey now--

EMMA
You heard right!

JACK
I'll be there in ten minutes.

EMMA
Okay. See you then.

JACK
Bye.

SOUND: THE CELL PHONE CALL CLICKS OFF.

SOUND: A POLICE SIREN ROARS.

SOUND: A CAR COMES TO A STOP.

SOUND: JACK SIGHS NERVOUSLY.

MUSIC: FADES OUT.

SOUND: A COUPLE OF TAPS ON A WINDOW.

SOUND: AN ELECTRIC WINDOW DESCENDS.

                    POLICE OFFICER
License and registration.

    SOUND: PAPERS SHUFFLE.

                    POLICE OFFICER (cont'd)
Thank you.
          (beat)
Brayden. I gave you a warning for running a
yellow light a few months ago.

                    JACK
What seems to be the trouble, officer?

                    POLICE OFFICER
Your taillights are out.

                    JACK
Really? I just had them fixed.

    SOUND: A PAPER RUSTLES.

                    POLICE OFFICER
You work for Mansfield Jewelry?

                    JACK
Yes. How did you know?

                    POLICE OFFICER
They provided the station with a list of
their employees.
          (MORE)

6.

                    POLICE OFFICER (cont'd)
Could you step out of the car and open your
trunk, please?

                    JACK
Why, officer?

                    POLICE OFFICER
Just do it.

                    JACK
All right.

    SOUND: A CAR ENGINE TURNS OFF.

    SOUND: A CAR DOOR OPENS.

    SOUND: FEET STEP ONTO PAVEMENT.

    SOUND: A CAR DOOR SHUTS.

    SOUND: FOOTSTEPS.

    SOUND: A CAR TRUNK OPENS.

    SOUND: PLASTIC BAGS RUSTLE.

                    POLICE OFFICER
Why are there two bags of silver and gold
rings in your trunk?

                    JACK
I-- don't know.

                    POLICE OFFICER
They fit the description of the ones that were
stolen from the jewelry store.

                    JACK
It wasn't me.

7.

SOUND: A CAR TRUNK LID SLAMS SHUT.

                    POLICE OFFICER
Put your hands behind your back.

SOUND: HANDCUFFS CLASP SHUT.

                    JACK
Please, don't do this. I didn't do it.
                    POLICE OFFICER
You can explain everything to the judge. Walk
over to my car.

SOUND: FOOTSTEPS TO A STOP.

SOUND: A CAR DOOR OPENS.

                    POLICE OFFICER (cont'd)
Get in.

SOUND: FOOTSTEPS.

SOUND: A BODY PLUNKS DOWN ON A SEAT.

SOUND: A CAR DOOR SHUTS.

SOUND: MUFFLED FOOTSTEPS.

SOUND: A CAR DOOR OPENS.

SOUND: A CAR DOOR SHUTS.

SOUND: A CAR GEAR SHIFTS INTO DRIVE.

SOUND: A CAR PULLS OFF.

MUSIC: SOMBER, UP AND OUT.

Software

Writing software automatically formats a script while you type. Most software includes features such as a character header name bank that remembers a name once it is entered for future use, a spell check, a thesaurus, and various report functions that are useful during the writing and production process. The leading software products are Movie Magic Screenwriter, Final Draft, and Fade-In. When using software, select the stage play template, which is consistent with the general audio-drama script format.

Determining Script Running Time

The way that a script is formatted helps to determine its running time. I recommend using the one-page-per-minute rule. This means that a thirty-page script, written using the general audio-drama script format, will have a running time of approximately thirty minutes. Most companies will accept scripts that use this approach.

Another way to determine script running time is by calculating the dialogue word count. This method is used primarily by writing staff members at companies that are required to hit a specific running time for each episode. On average, 144 dialogue words equal one minute of a produced audio drama. A thirty-minute script contains approximately 4,320 dialogue words. Page count does not apply when using this method.

Script Presentation

The visual presentation of a script creates an immediate impression on the industry professional who is going to read it. To make sure that is a positive impression, verify that you have included the three main components: a title page, a character page, and a script laid out in the general audio-drama script format.

Most script submissions are sent electronically to audio-drama companies. Once a script is finalized, create an official PDF version of it. For consistency, label the file using the following naming convention: "Script Title_YourName" (e.g., OnTheVerge_JohnSmith). Store all official submission versions of scripts in a single digital folder so they are easy to access when needed. Draft numbers are not included on the official submission versions of scripts. For guidance on how to handle draft information in file names for personal versions of a script, see the "Story File Organization" section of chapter 15.

A company may request a hard copy of a script on occasion. When this occurs, print a single-sided copy. If the script is thirty pages in length or less, fasten the pages with a staple in the upper-left corner. Scripts that are thirty-one pages or longer should be three-hole-punched. Put a brad or brass fastener in the top and bottom holes and leave the middle empty. Do not use color ink, graphics, or other elements on the title page or anywhere within the script.

Chapter 12

Collaboration

Collaboration is an important option to consider when you develop a script. Working with a co-writer makes it easier to set and meet deadlines, gives you a built-in story vetting process, and provides support when submitting to companies. Each of these increases the likelihood of getting a production.

Developing a script with another writer gives both of you the opportunity to grow. You can lean on your strengths and pay attention to how your fellow collaborator handles aspects of the development process that are not your strong suit. If you share the same strengths and weaknesses, it will make the writing more powerful in the areas in which you excel and give you an opportunity to work through challenges together. Discuss the ways that each of you tackle story development elements that you find tricky. You will both become better writers because of it.

Approaches to Co-Writing

The first step in a collaboration is to establish a way of working together. Discuss how each of you has developed scripts on your own. Identify the elements within your individual practices that you want to use in your collaboration process and then implement them. If you aren't able to come to a consensus on how to work together, there are a few options to choose from.

One method is to have each writer generate character and story ideas on their own. Set up regular meetings to discuss the work you do separately. When you agree on an idea, add it to a document that contains agreed-upon story points. At the end of each meeting, review the points to which you have agreed. Take stock of how much you have accomplished and how much work needs to be done. Continue generating ideas on your own and meeting to discuss them until you have fully realized and agreed upon characters and a story outline.

Another approach is to meet on a regular basis either in person or virtually. Brainstorm character and story ideas together. Discuss them and write down those upon which you agree. Work for as long as you are able to generate ideas, then stop for the day. If you use this approach, it will enable you to remain energized during all of your work sessions.

Consider having each writing partner do work that relates to their strengths and desires. If one member's strong suit is creating characters and another's is plot, assign those tasks to the given writing partner. Conversely, if each writing partner wants to create a specific number of characters and plot points, do so, then meet and decide which elements will be included in the story's concept.

Once you have developed characters and an outline, you are ready to write the script. There are several script drafting approaches to consider. The first is to meet in person or virtually and take turns at the keyboard writing the script. Discuss each line as you go. This incremental process will enable you to have a fully agreed-upon script when you are done.

A second method is to have each member of the team write a version of the script based upon the outline. Read each other's drafts on your own and then meet to decide which parts of each script will be included in the official draft. Once you have an agreed-upon script, read it separately. At your next meeting, discuss any changes you feel are needed and revise the script accordingly until each of you is satisfied with it.

Another option is to divide the outline in half. One member of the team writes the beginning of the script while the other works on the end. When you are done, combine your pages into a single file, then revise each other's work on your own. After that, read the revised draft and discuss what work is needed. Split up the tasks and revise the script until you have a draft with which both of you are satisfied.

Writers' Collaboration Agreement

When you develop an audio-drama script with another writer, you are creating an intellectual property that has legal and financial value. It is important to have an agreement that establishes your rights concerning the business partnership into which you are entering. This document should be signed by both parties, whether you are working with friends, family members, or business associates.

Lay out all terms clearly in your contract. A 50/50 split of ownership, profits, and expenses is standard. You can alter this amount on a case-by-case basis if needed. Be sure to itemize how the writing, marketing, and other responsibilities will be shared. Include a section that discusses how ownership of the project will work if your partnership dissolves prior to or after completion of the script. A well-thought-out agreement will help your working relationship run smoothly.

Contracts can be altered when needed. If your writing process, a specific financial aspect, or an ownership percentage changes after you sign an agreement, document it in an addendum and have both parties sign it. If you terminate your partnership, be sure to retain documentation that shows when the termination went into effect.

The only time a collaboration agreement is not necessary is when you are in a work-for-hire situation. If that is the case, be sure to sign a contract with your employer stating that in exchange for payment and other considerations, you are assigning the rights to your script to them. It is important to set up a clear work process and maintain open communication with your employer. Doing so will ensure a successful experience for everyone involved.

The collaboration agreement that follows is intended to be used as a guide to assist you in drafting your own contract.

Writers' Collaboration Agreement

This agreement was made in [insert the name of the city and state in which at least one of the parties live], by and between [insert the full name of writing partner #1] and [insert the full name of writing partner #2], henceforth referred to as the "parties."

The parties agree to write in collaboration an audio-drama script with the working title of [insert the current name of the script in quotes], henceforth referenced as the "work." The parties have chosen to establish all of their rights and obligations associated with the work within this contract.

Upon executing this agreement, the parties agree to the following terms and conditions:

1. The parties will collaborate in creating the work, which will be owned jointly once completed at a rate of 50 percent ownership for each party.

2. The parties agree to use a specific writing process, the details of which can be amended as needed by creating an addendum to this agreement. That writing process consists of the following aspects:

   a) Both parties will contribute equally (50/50) to the writing. Each will create story notes on their own and provide a copy of those notes to the other party. The parties will discuss their story notes and use them to create a master document of agreed-upon points about the characters, plot, and other story-related elements. [Tentative Completion Date: [insert date here.]]

   b) The parties will jointly use the master document of agreed-upon points to create an outline that tracks the characters and plot in a three-act structure from beginning to end. [Tentative Completion Date: [insert date here.]]

   c) Within a four-to-six-week time frame, the initial draft of the script will be written through a joint effort by the parties. [Tentative Completion Date: [insert date here.]]

d) All script rewrites and supplemental writings (i.e., query letters, log line, one-page synopsis) completed prior to the purchase of the script by an audio-drama production company will be written in a collaborative effort by both parties.

3. It is contemplated that a "submission ready" draft of the script will be completed by no later than [insert date here], provided, however, that failure to complete the "submission ready" draft by that date will not be construed as a breach of this agreement on the part of either party.

4. Upon completion of the "submission ready" draft of the script, it will be copyrighted in the name of both parties, and each party hereby designates the other as his attorney-in-fact to register such work with the United States Copyright Office.

5. If, prior to the completion of a "submission ready" draft of the script, either party voluntarily withdraws from the collaboration (which withdrawal must be confirmed in writing), then the other party shall have the right to complete the script alone, or in conjunction with another collaborator or collaborators, and in such event, the percentage of ownership, as set forth hereinabove in paragraph 1, will be revised by a written amendment.

6. If, prior to completion of a "submission ready" draft of the script, a dispute of any kind arises with respect to the work, the parties may terminate this agreement in writing.

7. Any contract for the sale or other disposition of the work, where the work has been completed by the parties in accordance with the terms set out within this agreement will require that the writing credit be given to the authors in the following manner: [insert all writing partners' names here in the order in which they will be credited in a production of the work].

8. Neither party may sell, or dispose of the work, or their share of it, without the prior written permission of the other party. That consent cannot be unreasonably withheld.

9. The parties agree that a mutually agreed-upon literary agent will be the exclusive agent of the parties for the purpose of sale or other disposition of the work or any rights therein, until such agent is terminated by the parties, or ceases to represent the work for any reason. The agent will have a six-month period in which to sell or otherwise dispose of the work and their commission for the sale or other disposition of the work will be 15 percent (15%).

10. Both parties agree to simultaneously submit the script to the following (lettered by priority):

    a) Audio-drama production companies
    b) Multimedia production companies
    c) Literary agents
    d) Retreats, fellowships, and grants

11. All expenses incurred by either or both of the parties in connection with the writing, registration, sale, or other disposition of the work will be prorated in accordance with the respective percentage of each of the parties as set forth in paragraph 1.

12. It is further understood and agreed that, for the purposes of this contract, the parties will share in, unless otherwise stated herein, the proceeds from the sale or any and all other disposition of the work and the rights and licenses therein and with respect thereto, including but not limited to the following:

    a) Audio-drama rights
    b) Sequel rights
    c) Motion picture rights
    d) Remake rights
    e) Television rights
    f) Stage rights
    g) Book and other media publication rights

13. If the work is sold or otherwise disposed of and, as a result, the parties—both or either of them—become employed to revise the work or write another media presentation thereof, the total

compensation provided for such employment will be shared by the parties in the same proportion as their ownership as set forth in paragraph 1. If either party is requested to be involved in such a revision but is unavailable (which unavailability will be documented by a written confirmation and signed by the unavailable party), then the party who is available will be permitted to do the revision and will be entitled to the full amount of compensation in connection with the revision work.

14. If either party desires to use the work, or any right associated with it, in any venture in which that party will have a financial interest, whether direct or indirect, the party desiring to do so will notify the other party and will afford the other party the opportunity to participate in the venture or in the proportion of the other party's interest in the work. If that party is unwilling or unable to participate in the venture, that party will have no further right of participation, or to any compensation arising from it, other than their proportionate share in the sale or other disposition of the work of that venture at its fair market value which, in the absence of a mutual agreement by the parties, will be determined by arbitration.

15. This agreement will be executed in a sufficient number of copies so that one fully executed copy will be delivered to each party. If any disputes arise concerning the interpretation or application of this agreement, or the rights or liabilities of the parties, those disputes will be submitted for arbitration and the determination of the arbitrator will be conclusive and binding upon the parties.

Dated _____ day of _____, 20__

_____
Signature of writing partner #1

_____
Signature of writing partner #2

_____
Address

_____
Address

Be sure to keep the original, signed version of your contract and any addendums in a safe place and store an electronic copy, such as a PDF, in your computer's script project folder for easy access.

Helpful Hints: Five Collaboration Dos and Don'ts

Dos

1. Determine what strengths you and your writing partner have and use them to the advantage of your partnership.
2. Establish an efficient collaborative process that works well for both parties.
3. Value your writing partner's contributions, whether they are used or not.
4. Have a signed collaboration agreement that establishes terms and expectations for each writer in the partnership.
5. Have a mutually agreed-upon exit plan that can be enacted if the partnership comes to an end.

Don'ts

1. Don't agree to third-party initiatives without your collaborative partner's knowledge and consent.
2. Don't stop listening to your writing partner. If you find that you have, determine what the cause is and how it can be worked through.
3. Don't push yourself or your fellow collaborator to overwork and become burnt out. To avoid this, take breaks when needed.

4. Don't parse out credit for specific contributions in your collaboration. Unless determined otherwise, all work is joint and should be valued and acknowledged as a team effort.

5. Don't stress out if contributions to the partnership aren't living up to what was contractually agreed to. If this occurs, discuss it so that a new understanding can be reached.

Chapter 13
Writing Groups

Once you have written a draft of your audio-drama script, it is important to get constructive feedback on it to help you fully develop it. Where do you go? Your first thought might be to show your script to family members and friends. While they may enjoy listening to audio dramas, most likely they won't understand the qualities that go into constructing them. Because of this, it is important to find an audio-drama writing group. There are two types: a small collective and a large, remote group.

Audio-drama writing collectives are intimate forums located within your town or county. Members become acquainted as they help each other develop their work and submit it to companies. Collectives usually meet in public places or take turns gathering at members' homes. Meetings occur one to two times a month. Script review tends to be done in one of the following formats. The first involves writers sending their scripts to each other so members can review them before getting together. In this model, meetings center around providing feedback. The second option is for writers to present their scripts at meetings. The presenting writer casts the roles in their piece with fellow collective members. They read them out loud and then provide feedback.

Large audio-drama writing groups operate online. They serve the same function as small collectives but have a broader membership. Writers in virtual groups exchange scripts individually when seeking feedback. As a member of this type of group, you should aim to get feedback from at least three writers before beginning a rewrite. That will ensure that you have a diverse response to your script. Networking in online groups is done on a one-on-one basis. Be sure to read member posts so you can get to know your fellow audio dramatists and reach out to those who work in the same genre or writing style as you do. Review any resources included on the group's internet platform. They can help you expand your knowledge of the field.

Finding an Audio-Drama Writing Group

There are several ways to find an audio-drama writing group. For small collectives, visit your local bookstore or public library. Ask the event organizer if any writing groups meet there. Audio drama is a unique form. You will want to be a part of a collective that specializes in it. If you are looking for a large group, consider joining Facebook's "Audio Scriptwriters." After you become a member, post an introduction and let members know what type of scripts you write, what you are looking for from the group, and how you plan to contribute.

Once you find an audio-drama writing group, it is important to determine if the group is a good fit for you. If it's an in-person collective, attend at least two meetings. The first will give you a feel for how the group operates. The second will enable you to become better acquainted with members and the inner dynamics of the collective. In large, remote groups, interact with members and observe their posts with one another for two to three weeks to gain an understanding of the tone of the group. Regardless of which type of group you join, you want to make sure that members give constructive feedback and want to help each other. If you find that either of these is not the case, it's best to keep looking.

Start Your Own Audio-Drama Writing Group

If you are unable to find an audio-drama writing group that works for you, consider starting your own. While this may seem like a daunting task, it is actually easy to do. Begin by approaching the event organizer at your local bookstore or public library and let them know you are interested in forming a collective. They will help you schedule time, provide a free meeting space, and make their patrons aware of your group. Be sure to advertise on websites such as Meetup.com, the local section of Craigslist under "writing jobs" and "writing gigs," and other free online writing platforms.

Arrive early on the day of the first meeting to verify that everything is set up and there is clear signage directing people to your meeting location. During the meeting, discuss what each writer is looking for out of the experience, set down some ground rules, and come up with a name for the collective. Leave time to get to know one another outside of your work as writers. If you find that you are the only one in attendance, don't be discouraged. Use the time to work on a script or peruse books and other resources. You might discover something that helps you as a writer or sparks new story ideas. Invite actors from local theaters to do cold readings of your scripts at meetings. Highlight this feature of the collective in your advertising. It may entice more writers to attend.

As an alternative to in-person gatherings, consider starting an online group that meets through a video conference app. Writing groups that hold meetings using this method function in the same way that in-person collectives do. Be sure to advertise the formation of the group in sources including the "Audio Scriptwriters" and "Audio Drama Hub" Facebook pages and the classified section of *Writer's Digest* magazine. To encourage connection between members, consider attending an annual audio-drama festival or conference together. That will give your collective incentive to go to the event and ensure that each of you knows someone when you get there.

Another option is to establish an audio-drama writing collective that interacts through email. This method works well if scheduling conflicts make it challenging to meet face to face. Guidelines for an email group can include monthly due dates for submitting script pages and sending feedback. Consider appointing one member to facilitate the script feedback exchange process to maximize participation and ensure accountability. During the first month of the group, ask each member to send the group a one-paragraph introduction. In subsequent months, encourage members to provide a summary of their writing accomplishments during the past month. This will enable you to get to know one another and learn from each other's experience in the process.

Script Critiquing Techniques

All writing groups should have guidelines for how to provide feedback on a script. If such a directive does not exist, it can be created. There are some core principles to bear in mind when drafting guidelines. Every script that is being developed has elements that work well and some that need further development. Ask members that provide feedback to start by discussing some areas of the script that are working well and then talk about aspects they feel need development. Feedback should be framed in a constructive manner. An effective way to do this is to have the writer who is providing feedback filter their suggestions through the lens of the story development tools discussed in earlier chapters of this book, such as character development, structure, world building, and dialogue.

Helpful feedback is specific. If the writer providing feedback simply says that the characters in the script need work or that the plot isn't believable, that won't give the writer receiving the feedback enough information to make meaningful changes. The writer providing feedback needs to explain why they feel a particular element needs development. They can provide examples that illustrate their point but should be careful not to tell the writer what to do. Using this approach will ensure that writers provide feedback that is useful to the writer that receives it.

Regardless of which type of audio-drama writing group you join, it is important to connect with other writers. No matter what stage of your career you are in, learning about the craft and marketing techniques that other audio dramatists use will broaden your perspective and help you evolve as a writer.

Chapter 14
Production

Producing an audio drama is a multifaceted process that consists of casting, rehearsal, recording, editing, and the release of the production. In general, an audio dramatist's involvement ends after they write the script. The more you understand about each step in the process, the better you will be able to serve the production through the work you do as a writer. Learning about the process also provides insight if you are interested in producing.

Casting

Once a script has been finalized, preproduction begins. During this phase, the company's producer selects a director to handle casting and recording. Some producers ask directors to cast from actors with whom their company has worked before. Others have the director send audition notices to various trade organizations and publications, such as *Backstage*. Auditions are conducted live or recorded and submitted electronically. They consist of an actor reading "sides," which are excerpts from the script that is being recorded. The director reviews the auditions and then chooses the cast for the production.

Rehearsal

Many companies rehearse a script before it is recorded. Rehearsals are held in person or virtually and consist of the director and actors reading the script and discussing each character's motivation as the story progresses. Some companies use this time to make minor adjustments to the script. In general, audio dramatists are not consulted regarding these changes. You can request to attend rehearsals. Doing so will enable you to handle any revisions that may arise. Companies that do not rehearse move directly to the production phase and make changes to the script as needed during the recording process.

Recording

Most audio-drama productions are recorded in person or virtually with the entire cast present. The recording of a series episode is usually done in a single session, while the recording of a feature-length piece is completed within two to three sessions. Prior to a virtual recording, the director will verify that all actors have comparable microphones to ensure consistent quality in recording. In the event that an actor is unable to attend a recording session, the director or a member of the crew will read their lines. The missing actor will record their dialogue later so it can be edited into the production. After the recording of each scene, the director asks the actors to rerecord any lines that were unclear or had artifacting (a technical glitch) in them.

Some companies use an asynchronous style to record scripts. This is accomplished by having each actor record their lines on their own and then send them to the director. The director reviews the recordings and asks the actors to rerecord lines as needed.

Editing

After the actors record their lines, the postproduction phase begins. The dialogue editor reviews the recordings and assembles the best takes into a rough cut of the production. During this time, actors may be asked to rerecord lines for clarity or to change their tone. In rare instances, an actor may be recast to ensure the strongest possible performance for the production. Once these steps have been completed, the volume level of all dialogue is balanced to ensure consistency.

Next, the producer reviews the script and creates a scene-by-scene list of the sound effects and ambient background noises that are needed for the production. They search through a commercially available sound library for effects that match their requirements for each noise in the script. Many audio-drama companies use a blend of prerecorded sounds and ones they create themselves if what they need is not available commercially.

After sound effects have been added, companies that use music have the producer review the cues in the script to determine the type and amount that is needed. Some companies incorporate music from the public domain while others hire composers to create an original score.

Once all layers of the recording are in place, the producer listens to the production. If it needs to come in at a specific running time, the length of the sound effects and music are adjusted as needed. After these edits are made, the piece is considered complete.

Cover Art

Each series or stand-alone production has its own unique cover art. This artwork appears as a thumbnail on the digital production file or is printed on the case if CDs are manufactured. Some audio-drama companies use public domain images, while others hire graphic artists to create artwork that will attract listeners to the production.

Releasing the Production

The final phase involves preparing the production for release. First, the recording is converted into a standard format that broadcasters, distributors, and publishers use, such as an mp3 or wav file. The producer then posts the recording on radio syndication sites, provides a copy to their podcast distributor, or sends it to a CD publisher, who packages it for retail sale. After these steps have been done, the production is released.

For more information on audio-drama production, see chapter 18, which features top leaders in the industry discussing their company's process.

Chapter 15
Support Documents, File Organization, and Copyrighting Your Work

Strong organizational skills are as important as craft is to a writer. Nothing is more frustrating than searching for a story idea, script draft, or piece of research and not being able to find it when you need it. Let's take a look at a few basic tools that can help you work more efficiently as a writer.

The Story Idea Bank

Ideas are the seeds from which stories grow. It is important to capture them clearly and store them in a single location or idea bank. When you have a new idea, write down as much as you know about it. Give it a title, a number to track it with, and note the date you created it. Be sure to state what medium you envision the idea to be written in (e.g., audio drama, screenplay, stage play) and the length (e.g., a short, a thirty-minute stand-alone piece, or a feature length.) This information will be useful when you are searching for an idea to develop.

There are several tools you can use to set up a story idea bank such as:

Notebook

Maintain a notebook or a set of notebooks that contain your ideas. Include an alphabetized index so you can easily find an idea when needed. Each listing in the index should contain the story title, idea number, and notebook number (e.g., "The Bayou Story," Notebook #3, Idea #297, Page #84).

Electronic Filing System

If you prefer to store your ideas digitally, start by creating a folder on your computer called "Story Ideas." Within that directory, save each idea as a word-processing document or PDF. If an idea has several documents associated with it, create a subdirectory within the "Story Ideas" folder to store the idea and all related documents. Label each single-file idea or subdirectory with the story idea number and title (e.g., 430_TheWaveBreaker).

Database

Set up a story idea database using a software such as Microsoft Access or File-Maker Pro. Include the following fields when configuring the database: story title, date of idea, idea number, and story idea.

Story File Organization

When you are ready to develop an idea into a script, create a directory on your computer called "Active Projects," then set up a folder within that directory labeled with the story's title. Move all documents associated with the idea into the story's folder. If you are developing a series to sell to a company, use the series title as the folder name. If a company has hired you to develop a single episode or a series, use the company name as the folder name.

Within the root directory for each story you develop, create the following subdirectories:

Correspondence

Save a PDF copy of each piece of correspondence here. For consistency use a file-naming convention such as PersonsName_CompanyName_Date_Time (e.g., TanyaLawson_RadioDramaCorporation_10-04-2021_10.45AM). This will enable you to locate a piece of correspondence when you need it. A second option is to set up a project-specific folder in your email app and move all related messages to that location. While storing emails in this way has value, you will need to maintain a separate directory in your computer's story folder for PDF versions of hard-copy correspondence.

Contracts

Keep a PDF copy of each fully executed contract associated with a project here. Maintain a central folder for hard copies of all contracts as well. Alphabetize the hard-copy folder by story title or company name and then by contract date, with the most recent contract on top.

Payments

Save PDF copies of invoices, checks, royalty statements, and receipts here. Label each file by its document type, subject, and date (e.g., Receipt_CopyrightFee_02-23-2023). Track your earnings and expenses associated with the script in a log. Columns to include are company name, date received, amount received, amount expended, and total earnings.

Productions

Store audio-drama production files here.

Research

Maintain an electronic copy of all research here. Consider using the following file-naming conventions for consistency:

- For *Books*: "Book_BookTitle" (e.g., Book_SwissFamilyRobinson)
- For *Book Sections*: "BookSection_BookTitle_SpecificSection" (e.g., BookSection_AudioDramaWritingHandbook_Pgs38-58)
- For *Articles*: "Article_ArticleTitle_NewspaperName_Date" (e.g., Article_1950sRadioTheatre_NewYorkTimes_09-10-1959)
- For *Interviews*: "Interview_InterviewWithInsertPersonsName_Date _MediaType" (e.g., Interview_InterviewWithJohnDoe_03-01-2023 _VideoRecording)
- For *Photos*: "Photo_BriefSubjectDescription" (e.g., Photo_HouseOn AHill)
- For *Videos*: "Video_BriefSubjectDescription" (e.g., Video_60MinutesSegment-SpaceFarming)
- For *Unique Document Types*: "Document_BriefDescription" (e.g., Document_JohnDoes9thGradeTranscript)

It is important to track research as you acquire it, so you know what you have and what you need. To accomplish this, consider creating a log that includes the following columns: document type, document title, date requested, document number, and document review status.

Within the "research" folder, set up a subfolder titled "annotated." Keep a copy of all research that has your personal notes on it here. Assign each document a sequential number. Enter that number into the "document number" column in your log next to the "document title" to which it relates, so you will be able to find it with ease.

Script Drafts

Store a PDF copy of each official script draft here. An official draft is a complete version of a script. Label the files clearly such as ScriptName_Draft-1.

Script Workups

A script workup is an in-progress version of a script. If you are developing a piece and have incremental drafts such as draft 1.1, draft 1.2, etc., these are considered part of the script workup for draft 2 of the script. Create a subfolder for each script workup. Outlines, working script files, feedback notes, and other development-related documents are stored in this folder.

Series Folder

Label the folder with the series title. Create individual subfolders for each episode you write. Consider labeling each subfolder using the following naming convention: "Episode-X.X_EpisodeTitle." The first X represents the season number, the second represents the episode number for that specific season. Store all documents related to a given episode in the related folder. (Note: This folder type is only used within a company directory.)

Writer's C.V.

A writer's C.V. ("curriculum vitae") documents every story you write a complete draft of, all your productions, awards, and more. It can be used to create a résumé, production histories, and your bio as a writer. The most effective way to maintain a C.V. is to update it each time a change occurs.

What follows are some key sections to include:

Education

List writing-related certificates and degrees you've earned, plus where and when you earned them. Be sure to include non-degree writing courses and writing-related internships.

Audio-Drama Productions

List each of your produced audio-drama scripts here. Include the title, year written, the company that produced it, the city and state where it was produced, and release information. For broadcasts, list the call letters of the radio station, the radio series title, the airdate, and the city and state in which the production aired. If the production is distributed by a syndicate, it may not be feasible to track all broadcast information. In this case, include the most comprehensive data you have.

Unproduced Audio-Drama Scripts

After you complete the first draft of an audio-drama script, add it to this section. Include the title and the year in which it was written. When a script is produced, move it to the "audio-drama productions" section and add production information to the listing.

Publications

Include the title, the publisher's name, and year of publication. If a script goes out of print or is published by another publisher, include that information as well.

Writing Awards

List the script title, the award name, which place it received, the city and state from which the award originated, and the year it was received.

Writing Groups

Enter the name of each writing group of which you are a member, along with the start and end date of your involvement with them.

Professional Organizations

List the writing organizations to which you belong. Include their names and the start and end date of your membership.

Writing Conferences

Input the conference name, the date you attended, and your role at the conference (attendee, presenter, organizer, etc.). If you were a presenter, list the title of the seminar you presented.

If you write in other forms, such as poetry, articles, screenplays, teleplays, stage plays, short stories, novellas, novels, or non-fiction books, include a separate area on your C.V. for each, structured similar to the "audio-drama productions" and "unproduced audio-drama scripts" sections.

Use the following example as a guide to help create your own writer's C.V. Note: bracketed dates represent the year in which the first draft of a script was completed.

Tom Thomas
P.O. Box 4547, Smith, NJ, 04321
(987) 555-0000, TomThomas@mail.com

Education
M.A. English Literature, Halstead College (2018 graduate)
B.F.A. (with honors) Dramatic Writing, Simpsonville University (2014 graduate)
Audio-Drama Writing Workshop (Littlewood College)

Audio-Drama Productions
The Audio-Drama Hub (half-hour audio-drama series)
Produced by James Wade for KVVZ 110.7 FM. Mitso Canyon, MT
Adaptation writer for:
Episode #1.11: "The Yellow Wallpaper" [2016]
First aired on 7/5/2016 (KVVZ)
Also aired on 6/27/2017 (WZPI)
Episode #2.16: "Make Mine Homogenized" [2013]
First aired on 4/28/2013 (KVVZ)
Also aired on 5/2/2013 (WCXX)
Also aired on 4/21/2015 (KDVQ)

Ants [2014]
Produced by Penelope Productions, Denver, CO as part of their "Original Audio-Drama Anthology" series, Episode 53. Released on: 10/22/2017

Unproduced Audio-Drama Scripts
The Trunk (part 1 - 2) [2013]
Pride and Prejudice [2018]
Laughter in the Rafter [2020]

Publications
The Blue Penny
Published in the anthology titled "Short Audio Dramas" by Audio Drama Scripts. 2015

The Rabbit Field
Published by Codi Dramatic Services, Cape Town, South Africa (5/17/2021)
Published by Border Press, Milwaukie, OR (4/2/2012) [Out of print as of 3/8/2015]

Writing Awards
Award Name: "2020 Best Short Audio-Drama Script" (Finalist)
Story Title: Cups and Saucers
Organization: The 54th Street Literary Society, New York, NY

Writing Groups
Prairie Grass Audio Dramatists (2010 - 2014)
Pens & Pencils Writers Group (2015 - Present)

Professional Organizations
The Authors Guild (2019 - Present)
The Dramatists Guild (2009 - Present)

Writing Conferences
Phillipsburg Audio-Drama Conference (Phillipsburg, NE) – 7/16/2015 to
7/19/2015
- Facilitator/Panelist for "Audio-Drama Writing" Panel, 7/17/2015,
  11 AM

Kansas Writers League Conference (Nork, KS) – 7/8/2014 to 7/10/2014
- Attendee

Aspen Writers Conference (Aspen, CO) – 6/22/2012
- Workshop Presenter for "Writing Dialogue for Audio Drama" 10 AM
  to 12 PM

Techniques to Find Time to Write

Creating an audio-drama script can be an exciting and rewarding experience. You get to take an idea and mold it into a story that has great meaning for an audience and monetary value as well. If the script on which you are working is not associated with a company, you will need to create your own deadlines to guide you to complete the project.

Writing takes dedication and a clear and focused mind. Time management is key. Set aside a portion of each day to write, even if it is only for fifteen minutes. Some days you may have more creative energy than you do on others. That's okay. If you connect with the script on which you are working each day, it will keep you in tune with what work needs to be done on it for when you have more energy to put toward it.

Use the time that you write wisely. Set goals, such as plotting out the story for thirty minutes or writing a certain number of scenes each day. Don't rush. Engaging stories take time to develop. The effort you put into your work will be well worth the time it takes in the end.

If you are writing for a deadline imposed by a company, a writing group, a contest, or other external entity, the need to complete your work in a timely fashion is more immediate. The development process, which includes plotting, outlining, and script writing, will enable you to create a clear rhythm in your work process that can help you meet a given deadline. Set up a writing schedule so you know how much you need to do each day in order to finish the script on time. It is equally important to incorporate the rest of your life into that schedule. Doing so will help you to balance all things you do, including your work on the script.

The Writing Completion Log

Sometimes as a writer it may feel like you do a lot of work but don't achieve anything. If this becomes the case for you, consider creating a writing completion log to help you gauge your productivity.

The log is easy to set up. In a blank document, insert the current year at the top of the first page. Add an entry underneath the year each time you finish a major phase in the writing process, such as an outline or a script draft. Criteria to include in each entry are the completion date, the script title, the document type, and the draft number. The log will show you how much you have accomplished in a given year and motivate you to do more.

Use the following example as a guide to create your own writing completion log.

2023

1/15   Completed "Skipping Stones" Outline – Draft 1

3/7   Completed "Housemates" Script – Draft 4

3/17   Completed "The Birdcall" Script – Draft 6

Copyrighting Your Work

Although you do not need to register your work for it to enjoy some protection, copyrighting your work is advisable. Several services, including those offered by the WGA, give limited protection. The United States Copyright Office provides the fullest benefits under the law. It is the service I recommend using. Benefits of registering a script with the United States Copyright Office include being able to sue for triple damages and have your attorneys' fees paid for upon winning a legal dispute. A copyright lasts for your lifetime plus seventy years. At that point, the copyrighted material falls into the public domain. You can copyright any script you have written and own. If a company asks you to write on a work-for-hire basis, the company owns the script. In this case, they have the responsibility to copyright it.

Electronic and hard-copy applications are available through the United States Copyright Office. The electronic submission process takes approximately ten months, while the hard-copy procedure takes up to eighteen months. If you file electronically at www.copyright.gov/registration, you will be able to track the status of your application online. There is no mechanism to track a hard-copy submission. Your work is said to have a copyright once the copyright office receives it. If you submit electronically, the copyright effective date is the day you submit your completed application. If you use the hard-copy option to file, the copyright effective date is two weeks after you mail your submission. The information entered on a copyright application is public record and searchable on the copyright office's website. Only include information that you want to be public knowledge.

After you register your script, you will receive a hard copy of the copyright certificate in the mail. Store it in a safe place. Consider scanning a copy and storing it on your computer in the script's directory, as well as in a general folder called "Copyrights." For consistency, label the file using a naming convention such as Copyright_ScriptTitle_CopyrightDate (e.g., Copyright_CrashingCars_11-28-2023). This will enable you to easily locate the certificate when you need it.

While the copyright year may be placed on the title page of your script at this point, it is not recommended. Companies want to read new scripts. By not including the date, your script will always feel current.

Chapter 16
Career Planning

Approximately 3 percent of all dramatic writers make a consistent living in the field. This leaves most writers constantly striving to secure employment. As you embark on a career as an audio dramatist, it is important to be mindful of this while you consider what your overall goals are. The personal career ladder can help.

The Personal Career Ladder

The personal career ladder is an easy-to-use system that will help you understand who you are as a writer, identify what your ambitions are, and enable you to decide which types of companies will be most fulfilling to work for. The first step is to understand who you are as a writer. To do so, ask yourself the following questions:

- In what genre do you write?
- Do the scripts you create use a specific style or storytelling method?
- Are there certain character types you tend to dramatize? If so, what?
- Do your scripts contain small or large casts?

- Are the stories you write geared toward niche or mass audiences?
- What theme(s) do your scripts explore?

Review your answers and take note of anything that surprised you. Perhaps you didn't realize that you tend to write epics, comedies, or intense dramas. Maybe you discovered that your scripts focus on one or two specific themes. Identifying the base characteristics of your work will help you define who you are as a writer.

The next step is to determine your ambitions. Give thought to the questions below.

- Do you write shorts, episodes, feature-length pieces, or a combination of these?
- Would you find more value in working for a small company that allows you to focus on the core qualities that make you unique as a writer, or would you prefer to dramatize story types, themes, and characters that a large company assigns to you that make you stretch as a writer?
- Do you want to use your work as an audio dramatist to move into writing for film, TV, or other media?

Your responses to these questions will help you gauge the kind of work you should pursue. Once you understand who you are as a writer and what your ambitions are, review the levels on the personal career ladder below and select the one that fits you best. All levels are of equal value.

PERSONAL CAREER LADDER

- Level I – Local audio-drama companies
- Level II – Lower-budget audio-drama companies
- Level III – Top-tier audio-drama companies
- Level IV – Major studios

Level I

Short adaptations and original scripts are produced at this level. The audio-drama companies are community-based and use local talent. Productions are broadcast on community radio stations or released in podcast form. There is no to little pay but a lot of opportunity to explore your voice as a writer and gain experience.

Level II

The focus on this level is on weekly, thirty-minute series that consist of adaptations and originals. Companies have a professional staff and employ writers on a per-episode basis. Productions are broadcast and available as podcasts. If you master a company's production style on this rung, you will be able to incorporate the qualities that are core to you as a writer into your work. There is pay usually in the form of a modest to moderate flat fee.

Level III

Productions include series and feature-length pieces. Companies in this category have a large fan base. Content is widely broadcast and available for sale. Writers work on a per-project basis or are members of the company's writing staff. With skill, you can integrate elements that make you unique as a writer into your scripts. Pay is either a moderate to high flat fee per script or a percentage of the sales for each piece you write.

Level IV

Writing jobs on this rung are diverse, highly competitive, and require the assistance of a literary agent to obtain. Production entities are comprised of major audio producers and film and TV corporations that use audio drama as an extension of their recent releases. Pay is lucrative and union rate.[1]

Developing an Action Plan

After you choose the level on the personal career ladder that best suits you, the next step is to compile a list of companies that are in line with your style and interests. Industry websites such as Audio-drama.com provide a central location to find producers. As you review each company's listing, be sure to listen to clips of their work and determine what they offer in a financial sense before deciding whether they are a good fit for you.

When you have identified at least ten companies that meet your qualifications, you are ready to move forward. Email each company on your list and inquire if they are looking for writers. Highlight your experience as an audio dramatist and offer to send samples of your work. If you don't find work through your initial list, add more companies and keep submitting until you connect with a producer who wants to hire you.

If you plan to move between the various levels on the personal career ladder, it is important to master the nuances of different companies' styles on a single level first. Doing so will give you dexterity as a writer. The more readily you can assimilate to a new style, the greater value you will be to a company you work for on any level.

If you are interested in writing on level IV, there are a few things of which you need to be aware. Most companies on this rung only work with writers who have agents. The first step toward getting an agent is to develop a diverse body of scripts and experience writing for companies at various levels. Once you have both, you will be ready to search for an agent. (See chapter 17 for the submission process.) After you sign with an agent, they will assist you in finding work with audio-drama companies or use your credits as an audio dramatist to help you transition into a career writing for other media.

Helpful Hints: Career Planning Pitfalls to Watch Out For

- <u>Uncertainty over what level to select.</u> If you are unsure what level on the personal career ladder to select, pick one that sounds interesting and explore it.

- <u>A level that is not a good fit.</u> If you discover that the level you are on is not satisfying to you, review the other levels on the personal career ladder and choose a new one to pursue.

- <u>Inability to advance.</u> If you are not certain how to advance on a given level of the personal career ladder, review the work being done by other audio dramatists at that level, then reach out and ask them questions about their journey. The information they share can help you find ways to move forward.

- <u>A level that is no longer valuable.</u> If you find that you are on a level of the personal career ladder that no longer has value to you, it is time to review the career ladder and choose a new level to pursue.

- <u>Inability to commit to a level.</u> If you find you frequently switch levels on the personal career ladder without getting a hold on one specific level, select a level and dedicate six months to explore it. At that point, assess your progress and satisfaction. It is important to note that success at any level may take time.

No matter what your goals are as an audio dramatist, review them from time to time. Doing so will help you determine if you are where you need to be. Regardless of where you work, it is important to remember, succeeding on any level of the personal career ladder makes you a success as a writer.

Chapter 17
Connecting with Audio-Drama Companies, Agents, and Publishers

Connecting with audio-drama companies, agents, and publishers is as important as developing a well-crafted script. When you are ready to start this process, there are two main tools you will need. The first is a query letter. The second is a résumé. It is also helpful to have a general understanding of how audio-drama contracts work. Let's take a closer look at each of these.

Writing the Query Letter

A query letter is a concise introduction usually written in the form of an email. There are three main uses for this letter.

The first use is to market an audio-drama script or series to a company or publisher. Companies receive a constant flow of emails, so it is important to use the subject line of your query to your advantage. Include one or two engaging phrases that highlight the essence of your project and encourage the reader to open your email.

Begin your query letter with a personal greeting to a specific person. If you are unable to find a contact name to whom to address your email, then use "Dear Sir or Madam" or "Hello."

The first paragraph should be a four-to-five-line synopsis of your project. The more intriguing you make the synopsis, the more likely the reader will be to request the script.

The second paragraph reveals the title, genre, story type (i.e., short, series, or feature-length), and any awards your piece may have won or placed in.

The third paragraph is your bio. Start by mentioning your audio-drama production credits and awards. If you don't have any yet, list your writing credits in other media or the titles of some unproduced audio-drama scripts you have written. Summarize any expertise you have related to the subject matter of the project you are marketing. End with your story development–related education and any professional writing organizations to which you belong.

In the fourth paragraph, ask your reader if they would like to receive a copy of your script or series bible. After that, close the email.

The following example can be used as a guide when you craft a query letter for a script or series.

Subject Line: Suspenseful, Audio-Drama Series about Friends, Rivals, and the Truth

Dear [Insert Name, or "Sir or Madam"],

When college-age, jewelry-store clerk Jack Brayden is pulled over one night by the police, several containers of missing silver and gold rings are found in his trunk. He claims he has no idea how they got there. The police arrest him for theft, forcing him to prove his innocence or risk losing the respect of his town, his academic scholarship, and most importantly, his freedom.

ON THE VERGE is an intense, new audio-drama series that explores friendship, jealousy, and the truth. The pilot script was awarded 2nd place in Scriptsmith's Audio-Drama Competition.

My credits include writing an audio-drama adaptation of Herman Melville's *Moby Dick* for the OPQ Company. CBA Audio Theatre recently released my original series *Fishing for Fools*. My feature-length audio drama, *Crashing Cars*, was a finalist in the Allegheny County Writing Competition. My stage plays have been performed throughout the Northeast. I studied dramatic writing at Middleton College and am a member of the Havenwood Audio Dramatists Group.

I'd like to send a copy of the series bible and pilot script for ON THE VERGE.

Thank you for your kind attention and consideration.

Sincerely,
[Insert Your Name Here]

The second type of query letter markets your skills as a writer to companies for potential work-for-hire opportunities. Clearly state the purpose of your communication in the subject line. Send the email to the artistic head of the audio-drama company.

Begin the body of your email with an informal greeting, such as "Dear George."

In the first paragraph, state that you are inquiring to see if the company is accepting audio-drama script submissions and if they need writers for current or future projects.

The second paragraph is your bio paragraph. It is similar to the bio used in the script marketing query.

In the third paragraph, close the email with a thank-you and mention that you hope to hear from them soon.

The following example can be used as a guide when you craft a query letter that markets your skills as a writer to a company.

Subject Line: Query on Audio-Drama Scripts and Writing Opportunities

Dear [Insert Artistic Director's First Name Here],

I am writing to see if you accept audio-drama script submissions and if you are in need of audio dramatists for current or future projects.

My credits include writing an audio-drama adaptation of Herman Melville's *Moby Dick* for the OPQ Company. CBA Audio Theatre recently released my original series *Fishing for Fools*. My feature-length audio drama, *Crashing Cars*, was a finalist in the Allegheny County Writing Competition. My stage plays have been performed throughout the Northeast. I studied dramatic writing at Middleton College and am a member of the Havenwood Audio Dramatists Group.

Thank you for your kind attention. I look forward to hearing from you.

Sincerely,
[Insert Your Name Here]

The third kind of query letter markets you and your work to literary agents to secure representation. This category only applies to audio dramatists interested in work on level IV of the personal career level. (See chapter 16 for specifics.) You will need to have credits at multiple companies and at various levels on the personal career ladder before seeking an agent.

On the subject line of your email, include a brief introduction. Whenever possible, send your query to a specific agent.

Start the body of the email with an informal greeting, such as "Dear George."

In the first paragraph, state the purpose of your email. After that, include a high-level view of your accomplishments as an audio dramatist.

The second paragraph is your bio paragraph. It is similar to the bio used in other query letters discussed in this chapter.

In the third paragraph, let the agent know that you would like to send a sample of your work, then close the email.

The following example can be used as a guide when you craft a query letter to an agent.

Subject Line: Award-Winning Audio Dramatist Seeks Representation

Dear [Insert Literary Agent's First Name Here],

I've reviewed the areas in which you specialize and feel we would be a good fit as client and agent. I have over a dozen credits in audio drama and am currently seeking to work for union audio-drama companies. I also have interest in using my experience as an audio dramatist to transition into writing for film and TV.

My credits include writing an audio-drama adaptation of Herman Melville's *Moby Dick* for the OPQ Company. CBA Audio Theatre recently released my original series *Fishing for Fools*. My feature-length audio drama, *Crashing Cars*, was a finalist in the Allegheny County Writing Competition. My stage plays have been performed throughout the Northeast. I studied dramatic writing at Middleton College and am a member of the Havenwood Audio Dramatists Group.

I'd like to send a sample of my work for your review.

Thank you for your kind attention. I look forward to hearing from you.

Sincerely,
[Insert Your Name Here]

Résumé

A résumé is a one-page listing of your top credits as an audio dramatist. It is laid out similar to a writer's C.V. and is submitted to companies upon request. Key sections to include are education, audio-drama production credits, and awards. See the "Writer's C.V." section in chapter 15 for more details.

How to Find Audio-Drama Companies

There are several resources that can help you find audio-drama companies to query. The most prominent is Audio-drama.com. It is a comprehensive directory of audio-drama producers and outlets. Each entry includes a link to the producer's website, where you can learn more about them, listen to samples of their work, and decide whether they are a good fit for you.

Individual audio-drama companies, such as Shoestring Radio Theatre and the Sonic Society, maintain information about other companies on their website. Shoestring Radio Theatre highlights several major companies, while the Sonic Society has an ongoing list of companies.

A final option is to conduct an internet search. Most community-based producing entities can be found in this way. Local producers are a valuable resource that may help you get your first production credits.

How to Find Literary Agents

If you are interested in securing agency representation, go to the WGA's (Writer's Guild of America) website and access their signatory agency list. All literary agents associated with the WGA have agreed to a general code of conduct, which includes not charging fees. Agents receive a commission of 15 percent of your earnings for each script they sell or each writing job they help you get hired for. That is the only money an agent receives. Research each agency to determine whether they are a good fit for you before submitting.

Tracking Your Submissions

Tracking your submissions is important. It enables you to know what script you sent to what company. Tools such as a spreadsheet, a word processing table, a database, or a hard-copy log can help you manage the process.

There are several fields that are essential to include in your tracking log. They are the company name, the company's website, contact name, email address, correspondence, and notes. For each submission you make to a company, enter the script title, what you sent (i.e., a query letter, résumé, or script), the date you sent it, and any future communications between you. If you are responding to a "call for scripts" ad, copy the text of the ad into the "notes" field. This will enable you to access the ad when needed.

The value of the data in your log will increase as you submit subsequent scripts because you will be able to see what each company's approximate response time is and their past responses.

If a company agrees to produce your work, note in your log that all future correspondence with that company can be found in the script's project folder. Save each new communication and the cumulative correspondence log for that company and project as a PDF file in the script's correspondence folder so all communications are available in one location.

Contracts

When a company wants to produce your work, they will request that you sign a contract. If a company does not provide a contract, suggest creating one so each party's rights are clearly defined and protected. There are two types of contracts that are used.

The first is a "buy out." A company will use this option when they want to purchase all rights to your script. Buy outs typically come into play when you write on a work-for-hire basis, such as if a company asks you to adapt a story from the public domain. Although the company will own your script, you retain the right to do future adaptations of the source material since it is in the public domain.

The second type is a "limited license" agreement. It gives the company the right to air their production of your script on their program and post it on their website. They are not allowed to make money from these uses. You retain the rights to future productions of the script. If the company wants to do more with their production of your script at a later date, they will need to negotiate those rights with you at that time.

Payment for both contract types will either be a onetime flat fee, paid upon acceptance of the script or a royalty based on the net earnings the company makes from the production. Royalties are typically paid to the writer twice a year.

Publishing

Publishing has the potential to provide you with ongoing opportunities for your audio-drama scripts, including stage performances, live broadcasts, and limited license recordings. There are two publication types.

The first type of publication distributes scripts for reading purposes only. Publishers in this category specify in the front of each script that production is prohibited or that anyone wishing to produce the audio drama must contact the writer directly to negotiate terms.

The second type of publication centers around production. It is the more prominent type of publishing for audio-drama scripts. In this case, the publisher acts as your licensing agent. They sell your script and collect production royalties for you. Standard contracts give the publisher 70 to 90 percent of script sales and provide you as the audio dramatist with 70 to 90 percent of the production royalties.

Publishers request either exclusive or non-exclusive rights to an audio-drama script. An exclusive agreement enables the publisher to be the sole entity selling your script. A non-exclusive agreement allows you to simultaneously publish your script with other non-exclusive publishers, which maximizes your sales and production potential. Non-exclusive publishers tend to be smaller companies that strictly publish digital versions of scripts.

Resources to find audio-drama script publishers include the Dramatists Guild's resource center, NYCplaywrights.org, and the playwriting section of the *Writer's Market*. Use the script marketing query outlined earlier in this chapter when submitting to publishers.

Helpful Hints: Five Essential Elements that Will Make Your Marketing Plan Dynamic

1. Personalize your correspondence with each company you contact to show that you are familiar with them and value their work.

2. Use active, aurally descriptive words in the story synopsis you include in your query letter. Doing so will demonstrate that you know how to write for the medium and will prompt a company to want to read your script.

3. Feature your most unique credits and accomplishments in the bio of your query letter. This will help engage the company in your work and writing ability.

4. Select a dynamic audio-drama script to use as a writing sample. For sample script pages, aim to have your sample, of no more than twenty consecutive pages, end in the middle of a climactic moment. This will leave the reader wanting more.

5. Be gracious when you follow up on a submission and include a new tidbit about you or your work that will intrigue the industry professional to want to read your work without further delay.

If you follow the practices laid out in this chapter, audio-drama companies will view you as a serious professional, which will increase your chances for production and publication of your work. Determination is key. Keep writing new material and submitting it to companies. That is the path to success.

Chapter 18
Insights from Other Audio-Drama Professionals

Understanding the nuances of working with individual audio-drama production companies is as important as understanding the craft of writing for audio drama. The following pages contain a collection of interviews with professionals from twelve of the leading audio-drama companies. Their discussion of craft, production, and marketing will give you insights into the industry, each company's brand, and the kinds of scripts they produce.

Atlanta Radio Theatre Company

Founded: 1984. **Location:** Atlanta, Georgia.

Website: www.artc.org. **Interviewed:** David Benedict (technician, writer, producer, actor),[1] Ron Butler (writer),[2] and William Alan Ritch (president).[3]

About: Atlanta Radio Theatre Company (ARTC) produces horror, fantasy, science fiction, romance, noir, history, and other genres. Their work includes adaptations of public domain stories from authors such as H.P. Lovecraft, H.G. Wells, and Jules Verne. They aim to work with living writers when possible and adapt their work in the way the author wants it expressed in the medium. ARTC shies away from excessive narration. Their productions range from five minutes to miniseries.

What are some essential tips writers should know about audio-drama writing?

David Benedict (technician, writer, producer, actor). Listen to all types of audio dramas and try to identify what works and what doesn't work.

Ron Butler (writer). Audio drama is people talking. Minimize narration (though it is sometimes essential). Monologues are tough and can sound contrived.

William Alan Ritch (president). Don't expect sound effects to be clearly understood without a setup. If you have a character driving a car, consider starting the scene with the car pulling away from the curb, then add some horns and traffic. Through this the audience will know that the character is driving a car.

What qualities make for an engaging audio-drama script?

David Benedict. Don't rely on your sound designer to create the environment for you. Detail what sounds you want to be present in your setting.

Ron Butler. Interesting plot and appropriate pacing.

William Alan Ritch. Characters are the most important thing. You need characters that the audience can love or hate, and a strong conflict. Don't monologue too much. Writers who aren't used to writing drama tend to put a lot of narration in. It was used in the golden age of radio, but not as much these days.

What are some essential qualities needed to craft a character in audio drama?

William Alan Ritch. Give each character a unique personality. If you use normal, everyday dialogue, it won't build character very well, but if you give a character little ticks or certain ways of speaking, they will have a unique voice. Interesting characters say interesting and surprising things. That's what people want to hear.

What qualities must a writer use to create a soundscape in audio drama?

David Benedict. A writer needs to be able to hear their script in their head. Listen to the world around you and try to imagine what it would sound like if certain sounds were missing. It's not necessary to create literally every sound that might be present in a certain environment, but knowing what's essential and what isn't is crucial. Nothing will take your listener out of your story faster than a sound that doesn't belong or an absent sound that should be there.

What qualities are essential in writing action sequences in audio drama?

David Benedict. Action sequences can be tricky because you want to convey enough information for the listener to know what's going on, but you don't need to have a blow-by-blow description. Complex acrobatic stunts like you see in action movies are often not appropriate and should only be used if absolutely necessary to advance the plot or define a character. In many cases, less is more, but in every case the characters should be reacting to what they're doing and to each other.

William Alan Ritch. Avoid excessive verbal description. It's a hard line to draw when you want to have the action be obvious to the listener and takes a lot of practice. If you're going to have a fight, a fist sound works well. People know, oh, they're in a fight. If you do something more subtle, you need to drop hints about it to clarify what's going on.

How can a writer best market themselves to an audio-drama company?

William Alan Ritch. Writers should start by looking for companies that are compatible with the kinds of scripts they wish to write. This involves listening to the existing output of a company and seeing if their material meshes with the stories the writer wishes to write.

David Benedict. After that, the writer should inquire as to whether scripts are being actively accepted. If submissions are being accepted, be open to constructive feedback and able to make any requested or recommended changes in a timely fashion. If the production company has not given a definite "yes," gently nudge those involved to see what the situation is.

William Alan Ritch. Occasionally, ARTC goes trawling for writers at science fiction and fantasy conventions, since that is our kind of material. I think more audio-drama companies need to find writers the way that we do. It behooves writers to proactively seek out companies at conventions as well.

What is your production process?

David Benedict. We use a workshopping process where a writer brings the first draft of their script in for a table read. They receive feedback, then revise their script and come back with a second draft. The number of drafts will depend on the commentary received during each reading.

William Alan Ritch. After that, we perform the script in front of live audiences at science fiction conventions to see what works. The audience lets us know when something's good or bad by their response. Then we make more changes to the script and possibly do more live performances, then more revisions until we have a script we really like.

David Benedict. Once the script is complete, we assign a producer and a director to do casting. Depending on the size and complexity of the piece, we may just assign roles to our stable of actors or we might hold auditions. We then go into rehearsals. For studio work, our rehearsal period may be somewhat brief because the script will be recorded over a series of days and the director will provide acting/characterization coaching during each of those sessions. We are able to do this because we have our own recording facility. Groups that have to rent studio time will want to have a much longer rehearsal period so that they can get in, lay down the tracks, and get out.

We schedule recording sessions based on who is available and which characters are needed for each scene. At this stage, a script supervisor is essential. The script supervisor is responsible for keeping track of which lines have been recorded and which ones still remain. If you are having to record scenes without certain characters and get those lines as pickups later, then a script supervisor is invaluable.

In terms of recording software, my philosophy is that what you use doesn't matter. Get a clean signal and use whatever you're comfortable with. After all tracks are recorded, we go into postproduction and soundscape.

William Alan Ritch. At that point, the producer and the director go through the recording individually and say, I think this should be a foley effect and that should be a recorded effect. A foley effect is when we go out into the field and record a sound ourselves. A recorded effect is taken from a hard disk that somebody else recorded. They tend to be things like traffic.

David Benedict. Once the sound effects are added, drafts of the production are sent to certain people (including the writer) for critical listening, and then adjustments are made as needed until the recording is considered complete.

Are there other aspects of audio-drama writing that a writer should know?

Ron Butler. A writer should be familiar with all aspects of audio production so they can avoid asking for things from the producers that are not doable, expensive, or awkward.

William Alan Ritch. Unless you're working on a major production, you are not going to get rich writing for audio drama. You have to do it for the love of it.

What do you see coming in the future for audio drama?

Ron Butler. The shift from office work to stay-at-home work will cut down on people listening to audio drama as they commute to and from work. That was a significant part of our market. On the other hand, podcasts have come to stay, and audio drama is a part of that genre.

William Alan Ritch. I think more companies will host YouTube audio-drama podcasts like we do. These audio-drama presentations use video of actors portraying the roles. You can make money from them.

Do you have any advice for new audio dramatists?

Ron Butler. The only way to learn is to make mistakes. Expertise in other forms of dramatic writing will help you with audio drama. Get used to varying script formats; everyone seems to have their own. Submit your best, most-polished scripts to prospective producers.

William Alan Ritch. Write what you know. That doesn't mean that you have to have done it. Just research it. I love science fiction and fantasy. Very few people have summoned demons, but you can research the legends to gain expertise in the subject.

* * *

Aural Vision, LLC

Founded: 2019. **Location:** Seattle, Washington.

Website: www.harrynile.com. **Interviewed:** Lawrence Albert (founder and producer)[4] and M.J. Elliott (writer).[5] **About:** Aural Vision, LLC is a reboot of the iconic, long-running Jim French Productions. They produce thirty-minute, period mystery series, including *Sherlock Holmes*, *The Adventures of Harry Nile*, *Murder and the Murdochs*, *Raffles the Gentleman Thief*, and *Hilary Caine Mysteries*. They also do stand-alone audio dramas in the H.P. Lovecraft style. Their audio-drama program *Imagination Theatre* is heard on more than 250 radio stations nationwide.

What are some essential tips writers should know about audio-drama writing?

Lawrence Albert (founder and producer). The first thing is logic. A script has to have logic. Even fantasy needs some logic, or you have nothing to hook your story on. Number two. How do you get people to keep reading after the first two pages? You need a good hook. It has to follow your story's logic. If somebody seeks out a detective after finding someone shot in the head, that's a hook. Number three. Don't include radio lines in your script. A radio line is when you're saying, let's go down to Bob's room. You hear footsteps, then, here we are at Bob's room. It's telling you what the action is instead of showing. If we can hear the wind, we don't need to be told the wind is blowing.

M.J. Elliott (writer). One: ensure that what you are writing is immediately understandable by your audience, but not in such a way that it appears unnatural. How do you make clear at the earliest moment which characters are participating in a scene, and where is that scene taking place without being obvious about it? Two: Brevity is everything. Perhaps the best advice I was ever given was "Can you tell the same story with half the number of characters? Once you've done that, can you halve that number again?" Three: Even the most minor characters have lives of their own. They're not just there to convey information. Think about who they are and what their individuality brings to a scene.

What qualities make for an engaging audio-drama script?

M.J. Elliott. A good pace. Just because a story is twenty-five minutes long, it need not be less satisfying than one told at an hour's length, or longer still. Once you have your listener's full attention, do not let it go. Make them laugh, surprise them, chill them, fascinate them with your deathless prose, but keep them interested.

Lawrence Albert. Fill your script with characters that feel real. Use unique traits, logic, and behaviors to illustrate who each character is for the audience.

What are some essential qualities needed to craft a character in audio drama?

M.J. Elliott. It's vital to know your characters inside. Don't make them boring. Remember that everyone has their own quirks, interests, unusual turns of phrase, things that make them sad or mad. Try to incorporate some of these elements into the characters in your script.

Lawrence Albert. When you craft a character who's not the main character, ask yourself, what is the purpose of the character? Where are they from? That's important because they are in your story for a reason.

What qualities must a writer use to create a soundscape in audio drama?

Lawrence Albert. Sound effects should support a script, not the other way around. Only use them when they are essential to communicate the story.

M.J. Elliott. The setting of one scene should be noticeably different from the previous one. If it's simply a matter of time passing in the same location (e.g., Baker Street, Later That Day), a musical break or a fade out and back in might do the trick, but for a change of location, background effects assist in informing the listener that the play has taken us somewhere else.

What qualities are essential in writing action sequences in audio drama?

Lawrence Albert. You've got to build into it. If you have a fistfight going on, the combatants can talk to one another leading up to and during the fight to bring that moment to life.

M.J. Elliott. Depicting action in audio drama is a fine balancing act, to let the audience know who's doing what to whom. I once read a script where someone shouted, "Take that!" each time they fired their weapon. Sound effects help a great deal to paint a picture, but it's the writer's job to provide clarification without being painfully obvious about it.

How can a writer best market themselves to an audio-drama company?

Lawrence Albert. They can contact the company and ask if they accept unsolicited scripts. If the answer is yes, then send a script. I would also suggest contacting literary agents. For small companies like us, we cut out the middleman. You can send to us directly.

M.J. Elliott. Patience is a tremendous virtue. Many months might go by between your initial contact with a company and any sort of response. You might, of course, receive no reply whatsoever. That happens; learn to live with it. Always remember that you're tailoring your material to any given producer's needs. Essentially saying to them, "I want you to turn my scripts into a series" won't get you very far, although I've seen budding writers do that. We'd all love a show based entirely on our own ideas, but that may not be what the producer requires or wants.

What is your production process?

Lawrence Albert. After a script is finalized, we cast it and then record it. We like to have the actors together in the same room and complete the recording in a single session. During postproduction, I insert sound effects from a library of thousands of effects I have into the production as needed. Music is then added. Once that is done, the piece is considered finished.

Are there other aspects of audio-drama writing that a writer should know?

Lawrence Albert. Always tell a good story. If you're trying to make a political or social statement, do not beat your audience over the head; wrap it around a good story.

M.J. Elliott. An ear for dialogue is impossible to teach, but vital to have. That's something you must learn for yourself, I'm afraid.

What do you see coming in the future for audio drama?

Lawrence Albert. There's a lot of podcasts out there. There will be a lot of opportunity in that area.

Do you have any advice for new audio dramatists?

Lawrence Albert. Don't talk about writing—do it. Find the story you want to tell and tell it. Understand that audio drama is a movie for the mind, and you have to help the audience in some cases, but you don't have to ladle it on top of them. Learn about dialogue. Write the way people talk.

M.J. Elliott. Prepare yourself for a lot of knock-backs. You will always have them, and they never get easier. Be aware that one producer's needs are very different from another's. There's no single right way to produce a script, and you must prepare yourself for the fact that you might be asked to write in a way that is not in your usual style.

* * *

Colonial Radio Theatre on the Air

Founded: 1995. **Location:** Boston, Massachusetts.

Website. www.colonialradio.com. **Interviewed:** Jerry Robbins (co-founder, artistic director, writer).[6] **About:** Colonial Radio Theatre on the Air produces audio dramas in all genres, including historic fiction, science fiction, drama, action-adventure, the classics, comedy, and musicals. Their popular western series *Powder River* ran for thirteen seasons and was adapted into a feature film. They have received numerous awards for their work.

What are some essential tips writers should know about audio-drama writing?

Jerry Robbins (co-founder, artistic director, writer). Keep the action moving; slow audio dramas can be hard to follow at times. People's minds can wander with long, drawn-out scenes. Be sure to introduce your characters into the dialogue by name. "Bob, glad you could join us." "Of course, John, what's the problem"—that's the idea, anyway. It doesn't have to be on their first entrance, but somewhere in their first scene. You only need to do it once, but be mindful of it.

What qualities make for an engaging audio-drama script?

Jerry Robbins. Good character voices that are unique. Not actors' voices, but what you write for them to say. Some may have certain catchphrases they use, others may speak with few words, some may swear, some may use slang, but each voice needs its own personality on the written page.

What are some essential qualities needed to craft a character in audio drama?

Jerry Robbins. It depends on the story. In *Powder River*, the lead character harbors a dark secret; he has no reason to live anymore—so listeners know he has no fear. He also has compassion and determination, so the listeners sympathize with him. These appear in many of my lead characters. So, I would say emotional undercurrent, compassion, and determination are essential qualities that are needed to craft a character for audio drama.

What qualities must a writer use to create a soundscape in audio drama?

Jerry Robbins. I think that falls to the editor. In my scripts, I kept it simple: SOUND: SANDSTORM; SOUND: LIGHT WIND, CREAKING FENCES, etc. The sound cue is one or two words—not long descriptions. Trust the editor; that's his job. Your job is to write the script.

What qualities are essential in writing action sequences in audio drama?

Jerry Robbins. Make sure the listener can follow the action. We had a *Powder River* episode with a saloon fight that lasted almost five minutes. The listener can easily follow all of the action. A different part of the room will have a slight volume change, but it's enough to get a visual "cut to" in the mind. Same thing with our production of *The Alamo* and *Little Big Horn*. I used direct sound cuts that were sudden changes in the action and volume. You still need to keep the sound you are cutting from in the background, so it doesn't sound like we are leaving the location—just moving to another section of it.

What is your production process?

Jerry Robbins. With *Powder River*, I would write the entire season of scripts . . . sometimes fifteen episodes per season, sometimes twelve. When I had about six scripts, I would schedule recording dates. The cast would assemble and record three or four episodes a session. We rarely used actors recording off-site, though we did on a few occasions—we just made sure we could match their microphones with ours so they would not sound "punched in."

After the season's episodes were recorded, the recordings were given to one of Colonial Radio Theatre's producers, who would do dialogue editing and add sound effects. I would review a draft of each episode and provide notes. Revisions were made to the episodes as needed. Then, the episodes would be sent to a composer, who would write an original score for each of them. When that was done, a graphic designer created cover art. After post-production, I would release the season through our digital distributor and our CD publisher for sale on a variety of platforms. The season would also be scheduled to air on several radio stations in the United States.

Are there other aspects of audio-drama writing that a writer should know?

Jerry Robbins. I try to set deadlines; otherwise you can go on forever with a script. Finish it, then read it aloud to yourself, not in your head, ALOUD. You will be amazed how some lines look great on paper but can be tricky or awkward to spit out. Rewrite them before the cast gets them.

What do you see coming in the future for audio drama?

Jerry Robbins. I anticipate that there will be a growth in the number of internet stations.

Do you have any advice for new audio dramatists?

Jerry Robbins. Keep at it and write as much as you can—every day, if you can. There isn't really an official script format to use. I've seen many different layouts from various companies. If a company hires you or asks for you to write a script for them, ask to see one of their scripts so you can write your script in a similar format.

* * *

Dagaz Media

Founded: 2018. **Location:** Portland, Maine.

Website: www.dagazmedia.com. **Interviewed:** Fred Greenhalgh (writer, director, producer).[7] **About:** Dagaz Media produces audio-drama adaptations of popular graphic novels, such as *Locke and Key*, *The X-Files: Cold Cases*, and *ElfQuest the Audio Movie*, as well as original works including *The Dark Tome* and *Of Fae and Fiends*.

What are some essential tips writers should know about audio-drama writing?

Fred Greenhalgh (writer, director, producer). Show, don't tell. By this, I mean find opportunities for characters to demonstrate who they are based on their actions versus what they say about themselves. Less is more. Complex, multi-person action sequences can work well in audio, but distill the point of view for the listener (e.g., in a battle sequence, focus on one person's experience of that battle; trying to do the big swooping shots they do in Hollywood movies will not work well). Silence can be as effective as sound. Give space so the subtle notes in your piece can be felt by the audience.

What qualities make for an engaging audio-drama script?

Fred Greenhalgh. Having a story worth telling is always paramount. Ask yourself, why are you telling this story? Why does the world need this story, now? Why is it an audio drama, instead of some other medium? A writer should have good answers to these questions, as they are the guiding compass for all other elements of production. There are limitless possibilities in audio drama—from realistic to fantastical, to very intimate to huge, complex casts. So, having a compelling story that is important to you, that only you can tell, is more important than trying to figure out what the "market" wants.

What are some essential qualities needed to craft a character in audio drama?

Fred Greenhalgh. Characters should have actionable traits that suggest their personality and help them stand out, especially in audio plays, where deeper levels of characterization (e.g., describing outer appearance or inner headspace) are difficult/clumsy to implement. Audio drama calls for greater diversity and inclusion. Characters of multiple genders make it easier for the listener to understand who is talking.

What qualities must a writer use to create a soundscape in audio drama?

Fred Greenhalgh. Honestly, I think the soundscape is someone else's job. The writer's job is to effectively convey the whole world of the story such that the next person who encounters the script during the production process can see the vision and help to create it. Unlike a novel, the audio play is not the final product. It's the blueprint to the house, not the house. But the blueprint needs to be clear enough that anyone can pick it up and figure out what kind of house should be built.

What qualities are essential in writing action sequences in audio drama?

Fred Greenhalgh. Clarity is key. It's easy to go hog-wild with sound effects, and much harder to figure out when to pull back and go with the subtle. Focus on the humanity of the story and not on the razzle-dazzle.

How can a writer best market themselves to an audio-drama company?

Fred Greenhalgh. Write a dang good script, and a pitch that makes the company feel like they must read it. Also, know your market. I can't count the number of writers who have sent me an unsolicited script that they pitched as if it was a totally original idea, and it was incredibly similar to something I'd recently seen.

What is your production process?

Fred Greenhalgh. Once you have a script you're happy with, cast it, record the actors, edit the voice recordings into a dialogue edit, then add sound effects and music. It's as simple and as complicated as that! I've used numerous workflows where either I did all of the postproduction roles or partnered with a number of people from all over the world, exchanging drafts of productions using cloud-based storage services. Postproduction can be a highly collaborative process.

Are there other aspects of audio-drama writing that a writer should know?

Fred Greenhalgh. They should know how to tell effective stories, how to cut things in a story that aren't working and that take away from the overall narrative, how to write dialogue that sounds like people actually talk. Audio dramatists need to have life experiences outside of creating and consuming content. Real life is where you get the raw material for stories.

What do you see coming in the future for audio drama?

Fred Greenhalgh. Right now, there is an incredible rediscovery of audio drama as a new age of the medium is dawning. There is so much good content coming out, and for once real resources are being invested in it. That means more competition, but also more opportunities. We are really just scratching the surface of what's possible. I'm incredibly excited to see a world where you don't have to keep telling people what an audio drama is and justify why it exists.

Do you have any advice for new audio dramatists?

Fred Greenhalgh. Make friends, learn, and try. Nothing will teach you more than making your first show.

* * *

The Icebox Radio Theater

Founded: 2004. **Location:** International Falls, Minnesota.

Website: www.iceboxradio.org. **Interviewed**: Jeffrey Adams (producer).[8]

About: The Icebox Radio Theater produces audio dramas about their corner of the world, Northern Minnesota. They have a separate podcast for horror, science fiction, fantasy, comedy, drama, mystery, and Christmas stories.

What are some essential tips writers should know about audio-drama writing?

Jeffrey Adams (producer). First, though obvious, remember your audience is blind. All necessary exposition has to be established somehow. Second, be engaging from the very beginning. Listeners have literally millions of options and won't give you more than thirty seconds of their time before deciding to listen further or cut you off. And finally—most importantly—WRITE IN SOUND!!! Tell me, the listener, what I am hearing. Don't fall back on methods from other art forms. "Int. Coffee Shop - Day" is fine for a screenplay, but I want to know what I'm hearing; the "ding" of a diner bell or the rumble of an espresso machine, the rough wallah of working men on their lunch break or the refined clicking of laptop keyboards underscored by Starbucks' smooth jazz creates a clear sense of place, which is unique and essential in audio drama.

What qualities make for an engaging audio-drama script?

Jeffrey Adams. Engagement always begins in the same place: character. If the audience doesn't know who these people are, they won't care about your story.

What are some essential qualities needed to craft a character in audio drama?

Jeffrey Adams. Voice (who is a character and how do they sound), main desire (what does a character want, why are they pursuing it, how far will they go to get it), and relationship (who is the character and what do they mean to the other characters in the story).

What qualities must a writer use to create a soundscape in audio drama?

Jeffrey Adams. First, the environment. If it's a realistic story it should sound accurate; a fantasy story should be filled with sounds that embody the world of that fantasy (but still adhere to some form of logic the audience can recognize). Second, some tones and sounds lead to certain emotions. Use tones and sounds that bring out the kind of emotion you want to inspire the audience to feel during a specific scene or throughout the piece as a whole.

What qualities are essential in writing action sequences in audio drama?

Jeffrey Adams. Ugh. Never easy in audio drama. In my humble opinion, words are completely undervalued in this area. I'd rather have a nice, descriptive passage of narration read with passion over a bed of action sounds (like a sword fight or a military battle) than an attempt to capture the soundtrack of *Saving*

Private Ryan's opening sequence. That just leads to a lot of people shouting and the audience wondering what the hell is going on.

How can a writer best market themselves to an audio-drama company?

Jeffrey Adams. Personal connection through various conventions and online communities where they can meet people looking for scripts. Also, consider producing your own script. It will be a fantastic education in the art form and bring you into contact with a lot of people. Producers are often more willing to respond to specific production questions than to 'Hey, anybody want to read my script?'

What is your production process?

Jeffrey Adams. Idea, then outline, then script. Edit the script for several weeks. We have an ensemble company, so I usually have actors in mind before I finish the script. Then schedule a table read. After the table read, schedule recording sessions unless another rehearsal seems necessary. Record dialogue and narration. Edit the audio files down to usable voice tracks. Go through the script and decide which sound effects need to be recorded and which can be utilized by existing recordings. Record sound effects if necessary. Lay all sound effects into the project with the vocal tracks. Add music. Do a final mix-down of the project. Create an MP3 file and post the episode to the appropriate podcast feed.

Are there other aspects of audio-drama writing that a writer should know?

Jeffrey Adams. Learn production. Scripts are not works of art; they're blue-prints for works of art, and the more the writer knows about their artform, the better.

What do you see coming in the future for audio drama?

Jeffrey Adams. More and better productions from a greater variety of sources. For the past twenty years, most producers have been independents and hob-byists. I think we're beginning to see the entertainment establishment dip a toe into the audio-drama pool. This trend will continue. Hollywood is always interested in making profits, and the low cost and quick turnaround time of audio makes the potential for profit very high. I expect to see more high-end, well-paying audio jobs in the future fueled by an ever-growing audience.

Do you have any advice for new audio dramatists?

Jeffrey Adams. Be curious, explore, and don't limit yourself because of fear. Be genuinely interested in people and why they do what they do. There's tremendous power in being the observer. And of course, write, write, write.

* * *

Pulp Radio

Founded: 2008. **Location:** Los Angeles, California.

Website: www.pulpradio.net. **Interviewed:** Roger Rittner (producer).[9]
About: Pulp Radio produces original audio dramas, adaptations of audiobooks, and adaptations of popular "pulp" fiction from the 1920s to the 1950s. Their work includes *The Adventures of Doc Savage, Bulldog Drummond—The Audio Adventure*, and *Charlie Sent Me!*

Roger Rittner's interview responses © 2022 Roger Rittner Productions. All rights, including reprint rights, reserved.

What are some essential tips writers should know about audio-drama writing?

Roger Rittner (producer). Have a strong story and play up the plot. The three-act structure of most plays (and film) applies to audio drama especially, because the listener must have a strong sense that the author knows where the story is going. Take the listener along for the ride and keep them in good hands.

Keep characters' motivations consistent. Character development is important, but don't rely on it alone to make a successful audio play. Character traits should be developed only to make the pursuit of the plot goal logical. Anything beyond that is just distraction. From the very first dialogue line, characters must have a central core of behavior. In some (especially a villain), the ultimate goal of the character may be hidden for a while, emerging as the plot develops. But a character's actions must never cause the listener to say, "Why the h— did he do *that*?" Introduce *all* the characters as soon as possible, preferably in the first act. (Agatha Christie was often criticized for introducing a new character right before the mystery's denouement, merely to rationalize the outcome.) All characters must support and advance the plot, or they're just window dressing. Keep the cast as small as possible, to avoid confusion (the author's and the listener's).

Be careful about "geography." Keep locations and physical relationships clear. Especially if you're writing a play to be produced in stereo, make sure characters are placed in specific dimensions. I often imagine that the characters are on a physical theater stage, with depth (front and back) dimensions as well as lateral (left and right) dimensions. I make sure their positioning and movement is spatially correct. I was adapting an audiobook in which the characters explored a deserted temple. The author hadn't been too careful about which characters were where, so they shifted positions without any motivation (or warning). When I got to laying out the recording script, I had to be very careful to keep them in logical positions. Specifying these things in the script helps the producer/director keep the action clear. Your best plot intentions can be ruined if the end result is geographically confusing. Bottom line: never do anything that would cause the listener to shake their head and say, "Wait a minute . . . Wasn't that character over there?"

What qualities make for an engaging audio-drama script?

Roger Rittner. It depends on what type of script you're writing. But remember, you're working in a sound medium. Audio drama relies 90 percent on dialogue. There are no costumes, no scenery, no lighting. The actors cannot rely on physicalities like facial expressions or body language. Everything depends on how you create plot and character through sound. Make your scripting specific, clear, authentic.

For an original script, tell a solid story and advance it through what the characters say, and their emotions as they say it. Create characterization through word choice and speaking style. Put exposition into words, and make it flow naturally from dialogue. Write dialogue that sounds like people actually speak. It depends on setting and historical period, of course, but within their given role, characters should sound natural to the listener. In general, keep words short, use contractions, be direct.

If you're adapting a book, it's probably heavy on narration. Find places where you can turn the narration into character dialogue. Wherever possible, eliminate attribution ("he said", "she screamed"), and put the feeling of the character's speech into the dialogue description. In fact, I often take a narration (e.g., "He smiled at the thought") and make that into a dialogue description—cueing the actor to emulate the feeling with his/her voice. Find sound-effect and music opportunities where they might only be inferred in the book—or even if they aren't, but your creative ear hears them.

Adapting an existing stage or teleplay into audio is somewhat easier, since much of the dialogue is already written. But remember the original story develops on a dimensional stage and incorporates visual elements you can't. Your script must accommodate the necessity of those missing elements.

What are some essential qualities needed to craft a character in audio drama?

Roger Rittner. Decide what challenge you need to set before the characters. Only then attribute qualities to each of the characters that will provide an interesting struggle each must take on. Classically, each should have a character flaw that hinders their struggle to achieve the goal. Even superheroes must struggle. Remember: no struggle, no drama. So, invent some personal problem for each character that puts roadblocks in the way. Overcoming that character flaw is often as important as overcoming the plot's challenge.

Each character needs to speak authentically. The rube farmer doesn't speak like a Shakespearean actor (except for comic effect). The college professor doesn't use words like "ain't" or "gonna." Be aware of how each character's dialogue sounds. Strict rules of grammar may not apply. Remember, you're writing words that are meant to be spoken. Ask yourself, "Do my characters sound like real people?" Use short words, use contractions, use jargon (sparingly).

Finally, be careful about putting too much plot exposition or complication into dialogue. If a character starts reiterating plot points solely to move the story forward, they sound artificial. It'll be obvious to a listener that this is the author's contrivance, and the character becomes unbelievable. "If you remember, Charlotte, the bank was robbed during the day, and the thieves got away in a Buick roadster with the license number 853-1212. But we must be careful, because they also kidnapped our daughter, and are holding her for ransom at an abandoned airfield in Minneapolis." Dialogue such as this is deadly because it tells backstory that the characters already know. Create an authentic situation with authentic dialogue that moves the story forward. Be sure to follow the truism: show, don't tell.

What qualities must a writer use to create a soundscape in audio drama?
Roger Rittner. Sound effects must always support the action or enhance the story environment. Don't use sound for sound's sake alone. If a sound doesn't support the action, don't use it. Just because a character refers to a dog, we don't need to hear a dog.

In scripting, specify sounds that listeners expect and are immediately recognizable for what you intend them to be. As an example, if you're scripting a western and a character is carrying a rifle, specify that a gunshot is from a rifle. If a listener expects a rifle shot and hears a machine gun, it destroys believability. (On the other hand, don't be so authentic when it won't make a difference to the listener. The sound of a 1933 Bugatti roadster is different from that of a 1960s Porsche. But unless it's key to the plot, does the listener really care? It's just a car.)

Another key to good soundscape is to put most sound effects under the dialogue. Far too many directors let the sound effects come in too loud and go on too long. In general, I let the effect quickly establish, then fade it under dialogue. Sometimes I just sneak it in under dialogue. Specify this in the script.

Music is also an important part of an audio-drama soundscape. Some writers don't indicate music styles at all, leaving production teams to guess at what you want. Be specific about where you want music, and what feeling you want it to convey.

What qualities are essential in writing action sequences in audio drama?
Roger Rittner. Proper pacing. A chase sequence is different than a gunfight is different than a fistfight. The pacing is determined by the type of action, and the words and sound effects you specify. In general, use punchy words. Use plosives and words that start with consonants. Keep sentences short. Overlap dialogue. Don't let one character speak too long in any one speech. Let spoken intensity mirror the action. Action is enhanced through choice of words, and even pauses.

Time the action scene appropriately. Over too quickly, and the listeners feel cheated. Too long, and it gets tedious, and becomes obvious that the writer is padding the script. Establish the peril, drive dialogue to address the peril, consummate the outcome (either the hero succeeds or fails), and then end the scene.

Keep sound effects sparse and supportive of the action. The pace is fast, and you don't have time for lengthy sound-effect sequences. Emphasize critical action effects (gunshots, running footsteps, etc.) and go easy on backgrounds.

Specify appropriate music. Music under spy thriller action is different than music under western action. Your script should lead the director to use the proper music.

How can a writer best market themselves to an audio-drama company?

Roger Rittner. Know your market. Study the company to which you want to submit and understand what they produce. Do they primarily produce mysteries? Or heavy dramas? Are they light on westerns? Maybe they're looking for one. If possible, contact someone there and ask about how to submit a script. Establish your credentials early.

What is your production process?

Roger Rittner. Once a script is ready for preproduction, I (as director) create rundown sheets that list every page in the script in which a certain character appears. This helps in scheduling actors so they are only called for the time their pages are to be recorded.

I mail the scripts out to the actors ahead of time. I include the entire script (not just "sides"), so the actor gets a sense of the complete story, and motivations for their scenes are clear.

I usually schedule only one actor to record at a time, since even two actors recording together adds more than twice the studio time. (A side note: I only use experienced voice actors or talented amateurs who can give good performances. This creates more work for me in postproduction, to stitch all the parts together. But it saves on studio time [and cost] and respects the actors' time commitment.)

Once in the studio, we record each actor's lines straight through. Retakes are recorded immediately, while the actor's mindset is still on the current scene. I tell the recording engineer to keep every take. Once I get into postproduction, I often find that what was previously not the best take, still fits into the flow of the scene better.

I used to have a sound-effects artist in studio, adding effects in real time as we recorded. Ultimately, I found that the extra time it takes to set up the effects for each scene, do a run-through, do retakes, etc. takes more time than the final product is worth. Also, sound effects are now inextricably linked to the dialogue in the recording, and tweaking timing, sound level, etc., is much harder. In the end, I have a large library of sound effects on disc and computer that are easily dropped into place during post.

Back at my postproduction studio, I load all the dialogue takes into a digital editing program and place each actor's separate speeches into sequence. Since I produce in stereo and put all dialogue on as many separate tracks as necessary in the app, it's easy to find just the right timing for everything. And since the engineer has provided me with every take (even some flubbed ones), I have choices as to which set of speeches sound best together.

Sometimes I add sound effects and music at the same time I assemble the dialogue tracks. Other times, I do all the dialogue assembly first, then go back and add sound and music, rearranging dialogue to fit the timing. It all depends on the complexity of the dialogue and soundscape I want to achieve. This is where my insistence on good "geography" is important. I can place the actors and sound on the audio stage precisely, so nothing is out of alignment with the listener's experience.

Finally, I go back and listen to the whole piece straight through. Lots of tweaking goes on here. The timing and interplay that sounded okay on first assembly invariably can be improved by listening in real time.

Are there other aspects of audio-drama writing that a writer should know?
Roger Rittner. First of all, study, study, study. Read up on drama as an art, independent of whether it's for film, TV, or audio. Listen to good audio drama until you can get "behind the sound" and tell when a script is good and when it isn't. Study script structure and formatting, and practice working with them until you can get the feel into your fingers and not be distracted by mechanics.

Avoid the temptation to edit and format as you write. Get all the words down, even if you think they're awful. Let creativity flow without filter. Much of it will be discarded eventually, but you'll have had the luxury of picking and choosing to create just the plot, characters, and atmosphere you want.

Do you have any advice for new audio dramatists?

Roger Rittner. Listen to good audio drama of the past, and study well-written scripts. Aside from my theater degree, most of what I learned about writing audio drama came from studying audio drama of the 1940s. *Suspense, Escape, One Man's Family,* anything by Norman Corwin. Even children's programs (like *Let's Pretend*) and detective dramas (like *Philip Marlowe*) can be instructive as examples of good audio structure. For continuously strong examples of plot development, look no further than *The Lone Ranger.*

* * *

Radio Theater Project (Washington)

Founded: 2010. **Location:** Mount Vernon, Washington.

Website: www.podcastplayhouse.org. **Interviewed:** Joseph C. McGuire (producer, writer).[10] **About:** Radio Theater Project produces a multi-genre, anthology series that features comedies, drama, and science fiction. In 2020, they began producing the stand-alone series *The Adventures of Scarlett Hood, The Mysteries of Dr. John Thorndyke, Richard Wade, U.S. Marshal,* and *Today's Life.*

What are some essential tips writers should know about audio-drama writing?

Joseph C. McGuire (producer, writer). Don't depend on dialogue only, and absolutely don't depend on sound effects only when writing an audio-drama script. Modern audiences want shorter scenes. Making dialogue sound natural is important. Observe conversational styles in life and incorporate them into your work.

What qualities make for an engaging audio-drama script?

Joseph C. McGuire. Each scene in a script needs to have movement. Not necessarily physical movement, but it needs to move the story forward.

What are some essential qualities needed to craft a character in audio drama?

Joseph C. McGuire. Get to know your characters so you understand how they talk and react in different situations. Characters need to have quirks. Each character's dialogue should embody the unique way they express themselves.

What qualities must a writer use to create a soundscape in audio drama?

Joseph C. McGuire. Dialogue is the most important thing in a production, but three kinds of sound support it. They are background, midground, and foreground sounds. Background sounds, which sometimes includes music, set the scene; midground sounds, such as opening and closing doors or footsteps, forward the action of the story; and foreground sounds, which are sharper sounds, add to the tension of the story. All three of these sounds work together to enhance the storytelling.

What qualities are essential in writing action sequences in audio drama?

Joseph C. McGuire. Tying dialogue to other sounds in an action scene will clearly illustrate the moment. Take a fight sequence, for example. You can incorporate a variety of concurrent action sounds, but you still need dialogue to enhance what's going on. In episode one of *Richard Wade, U.S. Marshal* ("On a Baffling Trail"), two characters ride in a stagecoach. They discuss where they are heading. Meanwhile, two other characters outside the stagecoach don't want them to get to their destination. They attack the stagecoach. The use of agitated dialogue and sound effects, such as hitting and stagecoach wheels accelerating, clarifies the attack for the listener.

How can a writer best market themselves to an audio-drama company?

Joseph C. McGuire. When you contact a company, express your willingness to revise your work to fit their needs. Writing is collaborative. Companies need to know that you want to be a part of that process.

What is your production process?

Joseph C. McGuire. Once a script is finalized, it goes into preproduction, which includes casting. For regular series, the main characters are already cast. You need to find the right actors for other parts. It's very important to include different kinds of voices, so they don't sound the same. Once the show is cast, it's ready for production. The first step in production is to record the dialogue. This is done in a virtual studio. Retakes occur after each scene is recorded. Next comes postproduction. All dialogue is edited into a draft of the production. Then you layer in the sound effects and backgrounds. This includes making sure the foreground, midground, and background are balanced. The most important part of the process is listening. I review each production many times and fix errors as needed. When this step has been completed, the production is done.

Are there other aspects of audio-drama writing that a writer should know?

Joseph C. McGuire. The writer's script plays a large role in audio-drama production. It tells other members of the production what they need to do to create a finished product.

What do you see coming in the future for audio drama?

Joseph C. McGuire. In its essence, audio drama matured to its final form in the 1950s. The telling of stories in the medium won't change much in the future. There might be effects to make it feel more "real," such as 3D sound and 360 audio production. Those are trends. In the end, the storytelling is all that is important.

Q: Do you have any advice for new audio dramatists?

Joseph C. McGuire. Start by listening to old-time radio and then listen to new audio drama. Old-time radio will give you a sense of timing. New audio dramas will give you insight into what types of storytelling techniques are current. Having people read your scripts out loud during the development process can be helpful. When crafting characters, listen to how people talk. Be aware of cadences, flows of language, and highs and lows of voice.

* * *

The Radio Theatre Project (Florida)

Founded: 2009. **Location:** St. Petersburg, Florida.

Website: www.radiotheatreproject.org. **Interviewed:** Jim Wicker (literary manager, actor).[11] **About:** The Radio Theatre Project produces audio plays in a wide array of genres, including comedies, mysteries, dramas, true stories, satires, and horror. They particularly enjoy producing noir and holiday scripts.

What are some essential tips writers should know about audio-drama writing?

Jim Wicker (literary manager, actor). Identify your characters by name early in each script and often so the audience always knows who's talking. Avoid narration unless it reveals the nature of the character who is speaking in addition to providing exposition (avoid outside narrators). Finally, and perhaps most importantly, listen to recordings of audio plays in order to gain an understanding of how they work.

What qualities make for an engaging audio-drama script?

Jim Wicker. Distinctive characters and dialogue, compelling conflicts, wit, and surprises.

What are some essential qualities needed to craft a character in audio drama?

Jim Wicker. Each character must have a distinctive manner of expression through vocabulary, phrasing, and syntax. A character should have a clear objective in the story. It helps if a character surprises us at least once in a script.

What qualities must a writer use to create a soundscape in audio drama?

Jim Wicker. Music should establish the tone of a piece. It is also useful as a bridge between scenes, signaling to the audience a change in time and/or location. Sound effects can also help to establish location as well as clarify action.

What qualities are essential in writing action sequences in audio drama?

Jim Wicker. When it comes to action sequences, dialogue is an essential complement to sound effects. They work most effectively hand in hand. For example, if a character named Margaret says, "How dare you point that gun at me, Robert?" just before a gunshot sound effect is heard, the audience will have a clear idea of the action that just occurred.

How can a writer best market themselves to an audio-drama company?

Jim Wicker. Many of our writers have responded to our ongoing call for scripts through the Dramatists Guild. I highly recommend the Guild as a resource for writers of drama. Also, check the websites of audio-drama companies before submitting to understand what kinds of scripts, show lengths, and formatting the company prefers.

What is your production process?

Jim Wicker. After the script is accepted for production, the director consults with the sound designer to determine the effects and music needs of the audio play. The director then casts the show using our company of actors. The day before the production, the cast does a read-through and tech rehearsal with the director and sound crew. The following evening, we perform and record the piece before a live audience. We do some postproduction work on the recording, then post it to our Sound Cloud site as a podcast.

Are there other aspects of audio-drama writing that a writer should know?

Jim Wicker. If you can, invite some friends over for wine and dinner (or at least snacks) and ask them to read the current script you're working on aloud.

You'll learn a great deal from hearing your dialogue out loud. It's both scary and a huge rush.

What do you see coming in the future for audio drama?

Jim Wicker. The growth of podcasts has been a huge factor in the expansion of audio drama. I think the sky's the limit now.

Do you have any advice for new audio dramatists?

Jim Wicker. Listen to many, many audio dramas. Then write about things that turn you on rather than tailoring your scripts to some perceived audience.

* * *

Shoestring Radio Theatre

Founded: 1988. **Location:** San Francisco, California.
Website: www.shoestring.org. **Interviewed:** Steve Rubenstein (co-producer)[12] and Monica Sullivan (producer).[13] **About:** Shoestring Radio Theatre produces a weekly anthology series of audio dramas featuring original stories and adaptations from all genres.

What are some essential tips writers should know about audio-drama writing?

Steve Rubenstein (co-producer). Don't have too many characters.

Monica Sullivan (producer). Don't do monologues.

What qualities make for an engaging audio-drama script?

Monica Sullivan. Keep the audience's interest by not having too many long speeches.

Steve Rubenstein. Let the characters carry the show.

What are some essential qualities needed to craft a character in audio drama?

Monica Sullivan. One of the best things to have in a character is humor. Humor always gets the listener's interest. Make your characters fun and make them believable.

What qualities must a writer use to create a soundscape in audio drama?

Steve Rubenstein. Don't overdo the sounds and music. Keep it simple.

What qualities are essential in writing action sequences in audio drama?

Monica Sullivan. Every visual cue needs to be illustrated by a sound. Don't make these moments too complicated.

How can a writer best market themselves to an audio-drama company?

Monica Sullivan. When you submit a script, don't try to sell it. Let the script speak for itself.

What is your production process?

Steve Rubenstein. After we select a script to produce, we give it to a director, who assembles a cast. We have three rehearsals and then a recording session. Next, we edit the recording, add music and sound effects, and put it on our website.

What do you see coming in the future for audio drama?

Steve Rubenstein. We see more emphasis on sound effects and overuse of music. While we use music and sound effects, we like the writing and acting to take center stage.

Do you have any advice for new audio dramatists?

Monica Sullivan. Keep at it. Don't give up.

* * *

The Sonic Society

Founded: 2009. **Location:** Halifax, Nova Scotia.

Website: www.sonicsociety.org. **Interviewed:** Jack Ward (producer, writer, host).[14] **About:** The Sonic Society is an audio-drama anthology series curated and hosted by Jack Ward and David Ault. Each episode features a production from a different company. The show covers all genres with an emphasis on productions from the United States and Canada. Jack Ward also writes and produces audio dramas for his company Sonic Cinema Productions (née Electric Vicuña Productions), as well as runs the Mutual Audio Network, a syndicate that curates audio-drama productions of all kinds.

What are some essential tips writers should know about audio-drama writing?

Jack Ward (producer, writer, host). Be aware that the story you write is going to be presented through sound. If you don't start with that mindset, you're more likely to confuse the listener than anything else. Limit your characters. The fewer there are, the easier the story will be to follow. Intrigue your audience through good characterization and plot that shows them the story and doesn't tell it to them.

What qualities make for an engaging audio-drama script?

Jack Ward. Each scene in a script needs to do one of two things: develop the character or drive the story. If it doesn't do either of these, it's gone. Keep your scenes fairly short. Some say movie scenes are two to three minutes long. In audio drama, it depends upon what kind of genre you're doing. If you're doing a fast-paced action-adventure story, keep scenes short, so that you can move from scene to scene to scene. Try to make each scene engaging enough that you're constantly driving either character or plot forward.

What are some essential qualities needed to craft a character in audio drama?

Jack Ward. The internal elements of a character that surface during a story are more important than a character's background. Create a character bio for each of the main characters. It will help you understand who they are and how they deal with things in different ways.

What qualities must a writer use to create a soundscape in audio drama?

Jack Ward. Soundscape is another character in your script. If any character takes up too much room, it destroys the story. My personal rule is that there needs to be enough sound effects to immerse the audience into the story without distracting them from the story. If you don't put any sound effects in, the production sounds flat. Your audience will wonder what's going on. It's a delicate balance that calls for a light hand to create the right blend.

What qualities are essential in writing action sequences in audio drama?

Jack Ward. Use specifics in your script. State that this happens, then this happens, then this, so the director knows what's going on and can communicate it to the actors. Be painfully slow, so there's no misunderstanding.

How can a writer best market themselves to an audio-drama company?

Jack Ward. Identify the audio-drama companies that are selling their wares and contact them about your interest in their work. Demonstrate that you understand and appreciate their products. Provide a portion of a spec script or a plot outline if asked.

What is your production process?

Jack Ward. After I have written a draft of a script, I put it away for a while. I find that the more distance I have from a script, the more critical I can be of it later on. When the script is finished, I cast it and negotiate pay. After that, the piece is recorded. I prefer to have the actors in one place when we record. That way they can get into their characters and feed off the energy of the other actors. This brings about the best performance. During postproduction, I do a rough edit of the show, where I pull out all the bad takes and rerecord lines when needed. Sound effects are then added. I have my own sound effects. Oftentimes things don't sound like you think they do, so you need to adjust the effects that you have. You have to consider ambient sound effects, direct sound effects, and plot-driven effects until you are satisfied with the sound. Once a scene is layered with sound effects, I send it to a composer. She builds music specifically for that scene. When the entire piece has been edited, I look for public domain pictures and modify them to create the cover art. Once I'm satisfied with the cover, I decide how to release the production. If it's a standalone piece, it will have its own feed on a website. I come up with a log line and a way to inform people about the production on social media, then I put that plan into action, and we're done.

Are there other aspects of audio-drama writing that a writer should know?

Jack Ward. There are some amazing things you can do by removing the visual component and forcing the audience to picture your story in their mind. For example, you could very effectively have an audio play of two or more parts of the body talking to each other. In my short *Night Driving*, I have two women fleeing in a car after murdering someone. In the end, the reveal is there is really only one woman in the car; the two voices heard were separate parts of her personality. While that can be done in other mediums, it can be done most effectively as a final reveal in audio drama because the story is entirely told through sound.

What do you see coming in the future for audio drama?

Jack Ward. As long as we have reasonably cheap ways to create podcast feeds, or some form of easily distributed media, audio drama will always have a place. It will be an uphill battle because audio drama requires trained ears in a way that people haven't been used to for almost a hundred years. Even so, it will always have a place.

Do you have any advice for new audio dramatists?

Jack Ward. Write your passion. Once you start a script, finish it. Don't be distracted by the next shiny thing in your eye. Find a story that you want to tell. Practice by telling everyone you know about it (that's something I do), and in the telling it will grow and develop so you can more easily write it. But finish it and get it out there into the world. Then go do the next one and the next one and the next one. Try different ways of transitioning between scenes. Look for new opportunities to introduce characters. Find ways to tell your message . . . even if your message is "have fun listening to my story"—that's still your message to get out there.

* * *

Spoken Signal Audio Drama

Founded: 2020. **Location:** Memphis, Tennessee.

Website: www.spokensignal.com. **Interviewed:** Robert Arnold (producer, writer).[15] **About:** Spoken Signal Audio Drama produces original audio dramas and adaptations in comedy, horror, and other genres. They were founded by the executive director and creator of Chatterbox Audio Theater, which operated from 2007 to 2017 and released over one hundred productions.

What are some essential tips writers should know about audio-drama writing?

Robert Arnold (producer, writer). Audio drama is its own thing and needs to be written in its own way. Imagine a scene of someone hiding from a pursuer who wants to do them harm. In film, this could be an intense scene with absolutely zero dialogue. In audio drama, you have to build the tension in a different way: Maybe an intense interior monologue, maybe two pursuers who are talking to one another, maybe the sound of the prey's quickening heartbeat. Hearing a character tell the audience information is awkward. It's always more dramatic to depict what the character does using sound to bring it to life.

What qualities make for an engaging audio-drama script?

Robert Arnold. For me, audio dramas need a certain amount of urgency. You need to capture the listener within the first thirty seconds. Anything beyond that, and you may lose them. It's important to maintain that kind of energy through the entire story. Really great audio dramas keep you on your toes. Stay one step ahead of the audience. If a listener knows where the story is going in the first few minutes of the production, they will get bored and tune out. You can't just write a story with all the standard rules and beats and expect people to get excited. Change it up. Surprise us.

What are some essential qualities needed to craft a character in audio drama?

Robert Arnold. Your characters need to have a distinctive voice. A really good script will use a character's word choices and nuances of language to give insight into the character. If a character is insecure, they will speak in a different way than a confident character. A good script will have that baked into the way the character talks, without having other characters say, "Oh, poor so-and-so, they're really insecure." A well-crafted character needs to be active. Besides language, diction, and word choice, character is revealed through action. If the stakes are high, a character will be forced to reveal themselves in the moment. If you've got a knight confronting a dragon, the audience will know whether they are a brave knight or a cowardly knight. No one will need to tell them. The most interesting characters are flawed. Create characters who are not perfect, who don't have the exact witty thing to say at every moment or are awkward or shy. The audience will be interested to see how they interact in the world, how they face this challenge or that.

What qualities must a writer use to create a soundscape in audio drama?

Robert Arnold. Be specific. Only include the number of sounds needed to clearly set up a situation or environment and no more. It's easy to get caught up in creating a richly detailed soundscape, but in the end, too much detail just distracts the listener from the story.

What qualities are essential in writing action sequences in audio drama?

Robert Arnold. Clarity is the main thing. You can have ten minutes of war sounds on a battlefield and no one's going to know what the heck's going on. Finesse in writing audio drama is keeping the listener up to speed without letting them know that you're keeping them up to speed. In a war scene, if there is a fight, keep it brief, have some chaos and then throw in some dialogue to clarify what happened. That's tough because it can slow a scene down. It needs to be done in an active way.

How can a writer best market themselves to an audio-drama company?

Robert Arnold. Know who you are pitching to. Chatterbox would have open calls for scripts every so often and I can't tell you how many old-time radio parodies we would get. They have their place, but we never did anything like that. If somebody sent that to me, I would know they hadn't been listening to our productions. Find companies whose work you like and with whom you feel a sense of kinship. Send them a script that fits their aesthetic. Send your scripts to people who want to see them. We got a lot of unsolicited scripts. If I didn't ask for it, I'm probably not going to read it.

What is your production process?

Robert Arnold. Once I have a draft of a script, I get several people to read it and give me feedback. I make revisions per the feedback I received. After that I do casting. I know enough actors that I can generally cast in my head. I don't do open auditions. I've tried it before and had mixed results. It's easier for me to work with people I know and trust. I have a small recording space in my house, enough for five people at the same time. We have at least one rehearsal before we record. I like to record with all the actors in the room together. We don't always record in order. I try to work it out maximizing people's schedules. I always record everything at least twice. It gives me options because there may be a blip in the recording or something may get deleted.

After the recording sessions, the project moves into postproduction. The first step is to do a dialogue cut of the show. Next, I insert the sound effects that are associated with the characters, so if a character walks from the left to the right and they're carrying something that's beeping and it needs to go left to right with them, I add that effect in at this point. Then I do a round with big effects like explosions and gunshots as well as atmospherics such as crickets or crowds, anything that glues it all together. Once that has been completed, I send the production to a composer to score it. I work with them to get to what I'm looking for. After scoring is done the production is released.

We release all our work as podcasts. Spoken Signal's work is on many podcast platforms as well as on our website.

Are there other aspects of audio-drama writing that a writer should know?

Robert Arnold. Don't chase trends. Tell the story that you want to tell. Good stories shine through no matter what the genre or style is. If you're just starting as a writer, start with something small. If you have a big world in mind, tell a small story from that world before you tell the full story. Make sure you finish a script, even if you're not totally happy with it. There's a certain amount of discipline involved in getting something from your brain onto the page that is viable, and that people will want to hear. Working through the hard parts is exactly how you learn and how you get better.

What do you see coming in the future for audio drama?

Robert Arnold. A phone or a computer is all you need to put audio-drama productions out into the world. People have started to realize that potential, and all of a sudden, it's exploded. There are stories being told all over the world from people of all different backgrounds and all different imaginations. It's incredibly exciting. I think in the future, we'll probably see a continued sort of Balkanization that we're seeing in other media. At the beginning, you had a couple of big audio-drama podcasts that made people go, "Whoa, this is cool. We can do this." Now that there are so many people producing, I'm not sure you're going to have that single show that sort of galvanizes the whole community anymore. The productions may never be blockbusters in the way they have been in the past, but there are going to be more stories and better stories. There will be more creativity, and there's going to be a lot to listen to.

Do you have any advice for new audio dramatists?

Robert Arnold. Listen to as much audio drama as you can, and that includes things like old-time radio that you may think are outmoded. Some of the original Mercury Theatre productions are a masterclass on how to adapt a novel into a one-hour audio drama. We as audio dramatists have a limited toolbox: only audio cues, dialogue, sound effects, music, and narration. Don't limit yourself any more than the medium has already limited you. Incorporate the storytelling techniques you hear in other productions into your work. Don't take anything off the table.

* * *

ZBS Foundation

Founded: 1970. **Location:** Fort Edward, New York.

Website: www.zbs.org. **Interviewed:** Thomas Lopez (producer, writer).[16]

About: ZBS Foundation produces audio dramas in genres including adventure, science fiction, fantasy, mystery, noir, and humor. They have worked with Allen Ginsberg and produced an audio-drama adaptation of Stephen King's story "The Mist." Their series, including *Jack Flanders* and *The Fourth Tower of Inverness*, were a cornerstone of the silver age of audio drama. The company continues to produce innovative work today.

What are some essential tips writers should know about audio-drama writing?

Thomas Lopez (producer, writer). Make sure your work is thought-provoking so that it adds to people's lives.

What qualities make for an engaging audio-drama script?

Thomas Lopez. It's all about the characters. Create interesting ones. Everything else hinges on that.

What are some essential qualities needed to craft a character in audio drama?

Thomas Lopez. Ask yourself who each of your characters is. Do you know them? I mean, really know them? If you don't, spend time with them. Listen to them! Don't write lines of dialogue for your characters—let them speak. They'll tell you what they want to say. Your function as a writer is mainly to be their editor.

What qualities must a writer use to create a soundscape in audio drama?

Thomas Lopez. Sound effects, music, environmental sounds, ambiance spaces, and the words to describe all of this.

What qualities are essential in writing action sequences in audio drama?

Thomas Lopez. Communicate each moment clearly through the use of sounds and dialogue.

What is your production process?

Thomas Lopez. I used to record in a studio, but now I send actors a recorder, and they record their lines at home. I edit the productions myself except for the music. I work with a composer for that. I use some recorded sound effects, but mostly I pull from a library of sounds I've created and recorded over the years. When a production is released, it is included in our weekly e-newsletter and posted on our website.

Do you have any advice for new audio dramatists?

Thomas Lopez. Life is short. Have fun writing and enjoy doing it.

Chapter 19
Resources

The following collection of resources is designed to assist you as an audio dramatist with everything from script development to the marketing process. Sources are organized alphabetically by topic and feature leading content in each area.

Adaptation Sources

Project Gutenberg – An online repository that contains full-text versions of thousands of stories, all of which are in the public domain and free of copyright restrictions. www.gutenberg.org.

Audio-Drama Conferences

Hear Now Audio Fiction and Arts Festival – An annual audio-drama conference that showcases various companies' work, offers production seminars, and provides networking opportunities. www.natf.org.

Audio-Drama Writing Awards

Austin Film Festival Fiction Podcast Script Competition – An award for audio-drama script writing. www.austinfilmfestival.com.

Marion Thauer Brown Audio Drama Scriptwriting Competition – An annual award for excellence in audio-drama writing. www.mtbscriptcompetition.com.

Minnesota WebFest "awards program" – An annual award for excellence in dramatic scriptwriting, including audio drama. www.mnwebfest.org.

Scriptapalooza – An award for dramatic scriptwriting, including audio drama. www.paloozapodcast.com.

Shore Scripts Audio Competition – An annual award for excellence in audio-drama script writing. www.shorescripts.com/podcast.

Copyright Information

United States Copyright Office – The government agency that oversees the copyright process in the United States and enables writers to register their work. www.copyright.gov.

Listen to Modern Audio-Drama Productions

Atlanta Radio Theatre Company – They produce horror, fantasy, science fiction, romance, noir, history, and other genres, including adaptations of H.P. Lovecraft, H.G. Wells, and Jules Verne. www.artc.org.

Aural Vision, LLC – They produce thirty-minute, period mystery series, including *Sherlock Holmes*, *The Adventures of Harry Nile*, *Murder and the Murdochs*, *Raffles the Gentleman Thief*, and *Hilary Caine Mysteries*. Their audio-drama program *Imagination Theatre* is heard on more than 250 radio stations nationwide. www.harrynile.com.

Colonial Radio Theatre on the Air – They produce historic fiction, science fiction, drama, action-adventure, the classics, comedy, and musical audio dramas. They have released over six hundred titles, including *The New Dibble Show*, *Ticonderoga*, and *Powder River*. www.colonialradio.com.

Dramafy – A streaming service that features high-quality, audio-drama productions from an array of producers. www.dramafy.com.

The Icebox Radio Theater – They produce audio dramas about their corner of the world, Northern Minnesota, as well as horror, science fiction, fantasy, comedy, drama, mystery, and Christmas-themed productions. www.iceboxradio.org.

KIXI – A radio station that airs modern audio-drama programs. www.kixi.com.

Mutual Audio Network – A syndicate that features modern audio drama and old-time radio productions of all kinds. www.mutualaudionetwork.com.

Pulp Radio – They produce original audio dramas and adaptations of popular "pulp" fiction from the 1920s to the 1950s. Their work includes *The Adventures of Doc Savage*, *Bulldog Drummond—The Audio Adventure*, and *Charlie Sent Me!* www.pulpradio.net.

Radio Drama Revival – They curate and host an anthology series. Each episode features a different audio-drama company's work. www.radiodramarevival.com/subscribe/#archive-feeds.

Radio Theater Project (Washington) – They produce an anthology series entitled *Radio Theater Project* and the stand-alone series *The Adventures of Scarlett Hood*, *The Mysteries of Dr. John Thorndyke*, *Richard Wade, U.S. Marshal*, and *Today's Life*. www.podcastplayhouse.org.

The Radio Theatre Project (Florida) – They produce an anthology series featuring comedies, mysteries, dramas, true stories, satires, and horror. www.soundcloud.com/radiotheatreproject.

Shoestring Radio Theatre – They produce an anthology series featuring original stories and adaptations from all genres. www.shoestring.org.

The Sonic Society – They curate and host an anthology series. Each episode features a different audio-drama company's work. www.sonicsociety.org.

Spoken Signal Audio Drama – They produce original audio dramas and adaptations in comedy, horror, and other genres, including the series *The Waverly House*. www.spokensignal.com.

Stay Tuned America – An internet-based radio station that features modern audio drama and old-time radio shows. www.staytunedamerica.net.

Voices in the Wind Audio Theatre – They produce original audio dramas and adaptations in the horror, mystery, suspense, and comedy genres, as well as programs geared toward children. www.voicesinthewind.ca.

ZBS Foundation – They produce audio dramas in the adventure, science fiction, fantasy, mystery, noir, and humor genres. Their work includes an adaptation of Stephen King's story "The Mist" and original series such as *Jack Flanders* and *The Fourth Tower of Inverness*. www.zbs.org.

Listen to Old-Time Radio Productions

Internet Archives – A free source that contains thousands of old-time radio programs. www.archive.org/details/radioprograms.

Jerry Haendiges' Olde Tyme Radio Network – A free source that has old-time radio programs. www.vintageradioprograms.com.

Mutual Audio Network – A syndicate that features old-time radio and modern audio-drama productions of all kinds. www.mutualaudionetwork.com.

Stay Tuned America – An internet-based radio station that features old-time radio and modern audio-drama programs. www.staytunedamerica.net.

Vintage Broadcast – Listen to free samples and purchase downloads of old-time radio productions. www.vintagebroadcast.com.

Literary Agents

Writers Guild of America (WGA) – The national labor union for writers who work in the visual and audio-drama formats maintains a comprehensive list of literary agents. www.wgaeast.org (services writers living east of the Mississippi River), www.wga.org (services writers living west of the Mississippi River).

Networking

"Audio Drama Hub" – A Facebook group for audio dramatists, actors, production professionals, and consumers.

"Audio Scriptwriters" – A Facebook group for audio dramatists.

Newsletters

Fiction Podcast Weekly Newsletter – A weekly electronic publication filled with news and opportunities associated with audio-drama writing and production. www.thepodcasthost.com/fictionpodcastweekly.

Organizations

The WGA Audio Alliance – A professional collective for audio dramatists. www.wgaeast.org/wgaaudio.

Produced Audio-Drama Scripts

Audio-Drama Companies

Atlanta Radio Theatre Company – Contact them directly to request a reference copy of any script they have produced. www.artc.org.

Websites

The Generic Radio Workshop – A website that contains html versions of old-time radio scripts. www.genericradio.com/library.

Old-Time Radio Researchers – A website that contains PDF copies of hundreds of old-time radio scripts. www.otrr.org/?c=scripts.

Books

The Baby Snooks Scripts Vol. 1 by Philip Rapp (author), Ben Ohmart (editor). Publisher: BearManor Media. 2014. This is the first entry in a three-volume collection of original audio-drama scripts from the old-time radio sitcom that starred Fanny Brice.

The Bickersons Scripts, Volume 1 by Philip Rapp (author), Ben Ohmart (editor). Publisher: BearManor Media. 2015. This is the first entry in a two-volume collection of original audio-drama scripts from the classic old-time radio series.

The Lost Sam Spade Scripts by Martin Grams Jr. Publisher: BearManor Media. 2016. A collection of original audio-drama scripts from the old-time radio series.

Powder River Season One Recording Scripts by Jerry Robbins. Publisher: The Colonial Radio Theatre on the Air. 2013. This is the first entry in a multivolume Kindle book collection featuring scripts from the series. (Note: Scripts from most of the six hundred–plus productions the Colonial Radio Theatre on the Air produced are available as Kindle books. See their website, www.colonialradio.com, for a complete list of their productions.)

Script Submission Opportunities

Audible Podcast Development Program – A division of Audible that develops and produces audio dramas. www.audible.com/ep/podcast-development -program?source_code=MRQOR22711102004JN.

Audio-drama.com – A comprehensive collection of audio-drama production companies and outlets. This is a powerful resource to review when you are ready to submit a script or market yourself as an audio dramatist to companies. www.audio-drama.com.

Dramatists Guild of America – The national organization for playwrights, lyricists, and composers. Their online resource center includes a list of audio-drama script publishers and producers. www.dramatistsguild.com.

NYCPlaywrights – A submission opportunity website that contains a section for companies looking for audio-drama scripts. www.nycplaywrights.org.

The Orchard Project – An organization that hosts free, annual script development workshops in various media, including audio drama. www.orchardproject.com.

The Sonic Society – They curate and host a weekly anthology program entitled *The Sonic Society*. Their website has links to most audio-drama companies whose productions have been featured on their show. www.sonicsociety.org.

Writer's Market – Writer's Digest Books publishes this submission guide periodically. See the playwriting section for a list of companies that produce and publish audio-drama scripts.

Script-Writing Software

Fade-In – A desktop software that contains an easy-to-use dialogue word count report that helps gauge script-running time. www.fadeinpro.com.

Final Draft – A desktop software that contains a two-step process to determine dialogue word count, which is helpful in gauging script-running time. www.finaldraft.com.

Movie Magic Screenwriter – A desktop software that contains an easy-to-use dialogue word count report that helps gauge script-running time. www.write-bros.com.

WriterDuet – A subscription-based software that contains an easy-to-use dialogue word count report that helps gauge script-running time. www.writerduet.com.

Notes

Chapter 1: Getting Started in Audio-Drama Writing

1. John F. Schneider, "The History of KQW and KCBS," *Voices Out of the Fog*, 1996, https://bayarearadio.org/sf-radio-history/kqw#:~:text=In%201949%2C%20CBS%20purchased%20the,on%20the%20air%20in%201951.

2. San Jose State Normal School, 1914 Senior Year Book (San Jose, CA: 1914), 70, San Jose State University Library Special Collections & Archives, https://digital collections.sjsu.edu/islandora/object/islandora%3A231_812, 6/20/2022.

3. Katrina Trask, *In the Vanguard* (New York: Macmillan, 1913).

4. Tim Crook, "Drama," *The Concise Encyclopedia of American Radio* (New York: Routledge, 2009), 228.

5. Erik Barnouw, *A Tower in Babel: A History of Broadcasting in the United States* (New York: Oxford University Press, 1966), 136–37.

6. Ibid., 137.

7. Tim Crook, "Drama," *The Concise Encyclopedia of American Radio* (New York: Routledge, 2009), 228.

8. Erik Barnouw, *A Tower in Babel: A History of Broadcasting in the United States* (New York: Oxford University Press, 1966), 137.

9. John Dunning, "Foreword," in *Tune in Yesterday: The Ultimate Encyclopedia of Old-Time Radio, 1925–1976*, by John Dunning (Englewood Cliffs: Prentice-Hall, Inc., 1976.), vii.

10. Tim Crook, "Drama," *The Concise Encyclopedia of American Radio* (New York: Routledge, 2009), 228.

11. Jim Harmon, *The Great Radio Heroes* (Jefferson: McFarland & Company, Inc., 2001), 17.

12. Erik Barnouw, *A Tower in Babel: A History of Broadcasting in the United States* (New York: Oxford University Press, 1966), 226.

13. Ibid., 226.

14. Jim Harmon, *The Great Radio Heroes* (Jefferson: McFarland & Company, Inc., 2001), 141.

15. Tim Crook, "Drama," *The Concise Encyclopedia of American Radio* (New York: Routledge, 2009), 231.

16. Erik Barnouw, *A Tower in Babel: A History of Broadcasting in the United States* (New York: Oxford University Press, 1966), 271.

17. Ibid., 273.

18. Jim Harmon, *The Great Radio Heroes* (Jefferson: McFarland & Company, Inc., 2001), 71.

19. David Wolinksy, Untitled interview with Jack Ward, Don't Die (blog), December 15, 2017, https://nodontdie.com/jack-ward.

20. Ibid.

21. Ray Barfield, *Listening to Radio, 1920–1950* (Westport: Praeger Publishers, 1996), 150.

22. Adam Graham, "Is a New Golden Age of Audio Dramas Coming?" *Great Detectives of Old-Time Radio* (blog), April 17, 2020, https://www.greatdetectives.net/detectives/is-a-new-golden-age-of-audio-dramas-coming.

23. Tim Crook, "Drama," *The Concise Encyclopedia of American Radio* (New York: Routledge, 2009), 230.

24. Jim Harmon, *The Great Radio Heroes.* (Jefferson: McFarland & Company, Inc., 2001), 91.

25. Erik Barnouw, *The Golden Web: A History of Broadcasting in the United States Volume II—1933 to 1953* (New York: Oxford University Press, 1968), 90.

26. Jim Harmon, *The Great Radio Heroes* (Jefferson: McFarland & Company, Inc., 2001), 65.

27. Erik Barnouw, *The Golden Web: A History of Broadcasting in the United States Volume II—1933 to 1953* (New York: Oxford University Press, 1968), 85.

28. Wikipedia; "The Mercury Theatre on the Air" entry, June 14, 2022, https://en.wikipedia.org/wiki/The_Mercury_Theatre_on_the_Air#Episodes.

29. Tim Crook, "Drama," *The Concise Encyclopedia of American Radio* (New York: Routledge, 2009), 230.

30. Erik Barnouw, *The Golden Web: A History of Broadcasting in the United States Volume II—1933 to 1953* (New York: Oxford University Press, 1968), 87–88.

31. Ibid., 153.

32. Tim Crook, "Drama," *The Concise Encyclopedia of American Radio* (New York: Routledge, 2009), 229.

33. Eric Rothenbuhler and Tome McCourt, "Radio Redefines Itself, 1947–1962," in *Radio Reader: Essays in the Cultural History of Radio*, by Michele Hilmes and Jason Loviglio (New York: Routledge. 2002), 367.

34. Barry Monush, *Lucille Ball FAQ: Everything Left to Know About America's Favorite Redhead* (Milwaukee: Applause Theatre & Cinema Books, 2011).

35. Eric Rothenbuhler and Tome McCourt, "Radio Redefines Itself, 1947–1962," in *Radio Reader: Essays in the Cultural History of Radio*, by Michele Hilmes and Jason Loviglio (New York: Routledge. 2002), 376.

36. Eleanor Patterson, "Reconfiguring Radio Drama after Television: The Historical Significance of Theater 5, Earplay and CBS Radio Mystery Theater as Post-Network Radio Drama," *Historical Journal of Film, Radio and Television* (New York: Routledge, 2016), 652.

37. David Wolinksy, Untitled interview with Jack Ward, *Don't Die* (blog), December 15, 2017, https://nodontdie.com/jack-ward.

38. John Dunning, "Foreword," in *Tune in Yesterday: The Ultimate Encyclopedia of Old-Time Radio, 1925–1976*, by John Dunning (Englewood Cliffs: Prentice-Hall, Inc., 1976), vii.

39. Eleanor Patterson, "Reconfiguring Radio Drama after Television: The Historical Significance of Theater 5, Earplay and CBS Radio Mystery Theater as Post-Network Radio Drama," *Historical Journal of Film, Radio and Television* (New York: Routledge, 2016), 655.

40. David Wolinksy, Untitled interview with Jack Ward, *Don't Die* (blog), December 15, 2017, https://nodontdie.com/jack-ward.

41. Eleanor Patterson, "Reconfiguring Radio Drama after Television: The Historical Significance of Theater 5, Earplay and CBS Radio Mystery Theater as Post-Network Radio Drama," *Historical Journal of Film, Radio and Television* (New York: Routledge, 2016), 654.

42. Ibid., 655–56.

43. "ZBS Brings Back Radio Drama," *Bluefield Daily Telegraph*, November 23, 1978, A5.

44. Jacob Smith, "Travels with Jack: ZBS's Post-Network Radio Adventure," *Resonance: The Journal of Sound and Culture* (Berkeley: Univeristy of California Press, 2020), 94.

45. "ZBS Brings Back Radio Drama," *Bluefield Daily Telegraph*, November 23, 1978, A5.

46. Wikipedia; "ZBS Foundation" entry, August 30, 2021, https://en.wikipedia.org/wiki/ZBS_Foundation.

47. Eleanor Patterson, "Reconfiguring Radio Drama after Television: The Historical Significance of Theater 5, Earplay and CBS Radio Mystery Theater as Post-Network Radio Drama," *Historical Journal of Film, Radio and Television* (New York: Routledge, 2016), 657.

48. Tim Crook, "Drama," *The Concise Encyclopedia of American Radio* (New York: Routledge, 2009), 233.

49. Eleanor Patterson, "Reconfiguring Radio Drama after Television: The Historical Significance of Theater 5, Earplay and CBS Radio Mystery Theater as Post-Network Radio Drama," *Historical Journal of Film, Radio and Television* (New York: Routledge, 2016), 659.

50. Jon D. Swartz and Robert C. Reinehr, "Introduction," in *Handbook of Old-Time Radio: A Comprehensive Guide to Golden Age Radio Listening and Collecting*, by Robert C. Reinehr and Jon D. Swartz (Metuchen: Scarecrow Press, 1993), ix.

51. Eleanor Patterson, "Reconfiguring Radio Drama after Television: The Historical Significance of Theater 5, Earplay and CBS Radio Mystery Theater as Post-Network Radio Drama," *Historical Journal of Film, Radio and Television* (New York: Routledge, 2016), 660.

52. Les Brown, "Radio Drama Makes Comeback in Wake of Popular CBS Show," *New York Times*, May 5, 1974, 95.

53. Eleanor Patterson, "Reconfiguring Radio Drama after Television: The Historical Significance of Theater 5, Earplay and CBS Radio Mystery Theater as Post-Network Radio Drama," *Historical Journal of Film, Radio and Television* (New York: Routledge, 2016), 654.

54. "Radio Soaper for Blacks," *Boca Raton News*, August 28, 1974, 5B.

55. Barbara Campbell, "Sounds of the City 1st Black Soap Opera," *Virgin Island Daily News*, August 21, 1974, 22.

56. Patience "Sibby" Wieland, "A Brief History of Audio Drama," *Medium* (blog), October 26, 2021, https://medium.com/acast/a-brief-history-of-audio-drama-5523475213f9.

57. Adam Graham, "Is a New Golden Age of Audio Dramas Coming," *Great Detectives of Old-Time Radio* (blog), April 17, 2020, https://www.greatdetectives.net/detectives/is-a-new-golden-age-of-audio-dramas-coming.

58. Tim Crook, "Drama," *The Concise Encyclopedia of American Radio* (New York: Routledge, 2009), 233.

59. Eleanor Patterson, "Reconfiguring Radio Drama after Television: The Historical Significance of Theater 5, Earplay and CBS Radio Mystery Theater as Post-Network Radio Drama," *Historical Journal of Film, Radio and Television* (New York: Routledge, 2016), 659.

60. Jacob Smith, "Travels with Jack: ZBS's Post-Network Radio Adventure," *Resonance: The Journal of Sound and Culture* (Berkeley: Univeristy of California Press, 2020), 108.

61. Patience "Sibby" Wieland, "A Brief History of Audio Drama," *Medium* (blog), October 26, 2021, https://medium.com/acast/a-brief-history-of-audio-drama -5523475213f9.

62. Tim Crook, "Drama," *The Concise Encyclopedia of American Radio* (New York: Routledge, 2009), 233.

63. "Voices in the Wilderness: Audio Drama in the Bronze Age," *World Audio Drama Day—October 30* (blog), October 20, 2021, https://www.audiodramaday .com/what-was-the-bronze-age-of-audio-drama-1995-2011-about/.

64. Tim Crook, "Drama," *The Concise Encyclopedia of American Radio* (New York: Routledge, 2009), 233.

65. Patience "Sibby" Wieland, "A Brief History of Audio Drama," *Medium* (blog), October 26, 2021, https://medium.com/acast/a-brief-history-of-audio-drama -5523475213f9.

66. Ibid.

67. Jack Ward, "Who Is Jack Ward in the Audio Drama World Anyway?" *The Sonic Society* (blog), February 2, 2019, https://sonicsociety.org/who-is-jack-ward-in -the-audio-drama-world-anyway.

68. Ibid.

69. "Voices in the Wilderness: Audio Drama in the Bronze Age," *World Audio Drama Day—October 30* (blog), October 20, 2021, https://www.audiodramaday .com/what-was-the-bronze-age-of-audio-drama-1995-2011-about/.

70. Leo Barraclough, "Shari Redstone's Advancit Capital Among Investors in Podcast Company Meet Cute," *Variety*, January 27, 2020.

71. Patience "Sibby" Wieland, "A Brief History of Audio Drama," *Medium* (blog), October 26, 2021, https://medium.com/acast/a-brief-history-of-audio-drama -5523475213f9.

72. Jack Ward (producer, writer, host, The Sonic Society), interview with author, August 30, 2021.

Chapter 8: The Story Development Process

1. Jacob Grimm and Wilhelm Grimm, "Hansel and Gretel." In *Grimms' Fairy Tales (translated from "Grimms' Kinder und Hausmärchen")*, by Jacob Grimm and Wilhelm Grimm, translated by Edgar Taylor and Marian Edwardes (Dehli: Lector House, 2001), 29–31.

Chapter 9: Adaptation

1. Philip K. Dick, "Beyond the Door," in *Fantastic Universe,* January 1954, 104–05.

2. Ibid., 104–05.

3. Ibid., 101.

4. Barry M. Putt, Jr., 2014, *Beyond the Door* script adaptation of Philip K. Dick's short story originally aired on the audio-drama series *Radio Theater Project,* Radio Theater Project.

5. Jules Verne, *The Mysterious Island,* translated by Stephen W. White (Philadelphia: The Evening Telegraph, 1876), 8–9.

6. Barry M. Putt, Jr., 2017, *Mysterious Island,* audio-drama adaptation of Jules Verne's novel, unpublished manuscript.

Chapter 16: Career Planning

1. Barry M. Putt, Jr., "The Business Side of Writing with Barry: Introduction to the Personal Career Ladder," *Riprap Entertainment TV Ezine,* June 15, 2007, www.riprapentertainment.com/barrybiz1.html.

Chapter 18: Insights from Other Audio-Drama Professionals

1. David Benedict (technician, writer, producer, actor, Atlanta Radio Theatre Company), interview with author, September 1, 2021.

2. Ron Butler (writer, Atlanta Radio Theatre Company), interview with author, September 29, 2021.

3. William Alan Ritch (president, Atlanta Radio Theatre Company), interview with author, October 8, 2021.

4. Lawrence Albert (founder and producer, Aural Vision, LLC), interview with author, August 31, 2021.

5. M.J. Elliott (writer, Aural Vision, LLC), interview with author, September 1, 2021.

6. Jerry Robbins (co-founder, artistic director, writer, Colonial Radio Theatre on the Air), interview with author, September 30, 2021.

7. Fred Greenhalgh (writer, director, producer, Dagaz Media), interview with author, August 30, 2021.

8. Jeffrey Adams (producer, Icebox Radio Theater), interview with author, September 20, 2021.

9. Roger Rittner (producer, Pulp Radio), interview with author, October 11, 2021.

10. Joseph C. McGuire (producer, writer, Radio Theater Project), interview with author, August 31, 2021.

11. Jim Wicker (literary manager, actor, The Radio Theatre Project) interview with author, September 21, 2021.

12. Steve Rubenstein (co-producer, Shoestring Radio Theatre), interview with author, October 6, 2021.

13. Monica Sullivan (producer, Shoestring Radio Theatre), interview with author, October 6, 2021.

14. Jack Ward (producer, writer, host, The Sonic Society), interview with author, August 30, 2021.

15. Robert Arnold (producer, writer, Spoken Signal Audio Drama), interview with author, September 14, 2021.

16. Thomas Lopez (producer, writer, ZBS Foundation), interview with author, September 1, 2021, September 2, 2021.

Bibliography

Barfield, Ray. *Listening to Radio, 1920–1950*. Westport: Praeger Publishers, 1996.

Barnouw, Erik. *A Tower in Babel: A History of Broadcasting in the United States*. New York: Oxford University Press, 1966.

———. *The Golden Web: A History of Broadcasting in the United States Volume II—1933 to 1953*. New York: Oxford University Press, 1968.

Barraclough, Leo. "Shari Redstone's Advancit Capital Among Investors in Podcast Company Meet Cute." *Variety* (January 27, 2020).

Brown, Les. "Radio Drama Makes Comeback in Wake of Popular CBS Show." *New York Times* (May 5, 1974), 95.

Campbell, Barbara. "Sounds of the City 1st Black Soap Opera." *Virgin Island Daily News* (August 21, 1974), 22.

Crook, Tim. "Drama." *The Concise Encyclopedia of American Radio*. New York: Routledge, 2009.

Dick, Philip K. "Beyond the Door." *Fantastic Universe* 1, no. 4 (January 1954): 101–06.

Dunning, John. "Foreword." In *Tune in Yesterday: The Ultimate Encyclopedia of Old-Time Radio, 1925–1976*, vii–xi. Englewood Cliffs: Prentice-Hall, Inc., 1976.

Graham, Adam. "Is a New Golden Age of Audio Dramas Coming?" In *Great Detectives of Old-Time Radio*. Accessed November 12, 2021. https://www.greatdetectives.net/detectives/is-a-new-golden-age-of-audio-dramas-coming.

Grimm, Jacob, and Wilhelm Grimm. "Hansel and Gretel." In *Grimms' Fairy Tales (translated from "Grimms' Kinder und Hausmärchen")*, by Jacob Grimm and Wilhelm Grimm, translated by Edgar Taylor and Marian Edwardes, 29–31. Dehli: Lector House, 2001.

Harmon, Jim. *The Great Radio Heroes*. Jefferson: McFarland, 2001.

Monush, Barry. *Lucille Ball FAQ: Everything Left to Know About America's Favorite Redhead*. Milwaukee: Applause, 2011.

Patterson, Eleanor. "Reconfiguring Radio Drama after Television: The Historical Significance of Theater 5, Earplay and CBS Radio Mystery Theater as Post-Network Radio Drama," *Historical Journal of Film, Radio and Television* 36, no. 4 (2016): 649–67. http://dx.doi.org/ 10.1080/ 01439685.2016.1 157287.

Putt, Barry M. Jr. "The Business Side of Writing with Barry: Introduction to the Personal Career Ladder." *Riprap Entertainment TV Ezine*. Accessed June 15, 2007. www.riprapentertainment.com/barrybiz1.html.

———. *Beyond the Door*, script adaptation of Philip K. Dick's short story originally aired on the audio-drama series *Radio Theater Project*. Radio Theater Project. 2014.

———. *Mysterious Island*. audio-drama adaptation of Jules Verne's novel. Unpublished manuscript. 2017.

"Radio Soaper for Blacks." *Boca Raton News* (August 28, 1974), 5B.

Rothenbuhler, Eric, and Tome McCourt. "Radio Redefines Itself, 1947–1962." In *Radio Reader: Essays in the Cultural History of Radio*, edited by Jason Loviglio and Michele Hilmes, 367–87. New York: Routledge, 2002.

San Jose State Normal School. 1914 Senior Year Book. San Jose, CA: 1914. San Jose State University Library Special Collections & Archives, https://digitalcollections.sjsu.edu/islandora/object/islandora%3A231_812.

Schneider, John F. "The History of KQW and KCBS." *Voices Out of the Fog*. Accessed June 18, 2022. https://bayarearadio.org/sf-radio-history/kqw#:~:text=In%201949%2C%20CBS%20purchased%20the,on%20the%20air%20in%201951.

Smith, Jacob. "Travels with Jack: ZBS's Post-Network Radio Adventure." *Resonance: The Journal of Sound and Culture* 1, no. 1 (2020): 94–115.

Swartz, Jon D., and Robert C. Reinehr. "Introduction." In *Handbook of Old-Time Radio: A Comprehensive Guide to Golden Age Radio Listening and Collecting*, edited by Jon D. Swartz and Robert C. Reinehr, ix–xv. Metuchen: Scarecrow Press, 1993.

Trask, Katrina. *In the Vanguard*. New York: Macmillan, 1913.

Verne, Jules. *The Mysterious Island*, translated by Stephen W. White. Philadelphia: The Evening Telegraph, 1876.

"Voices in the Wilderness: Audio Drama in the Bronze Age." *World Audio Drama Day—October 30*. Accessed October 20, 2021. https://www.audiodramaday.com/what-was-the-bronze-age-of-audio-drama-1995-2011-about/.

Ward, Jack. "Who Is Jack Ward in the Audio Drama World Anyway?" *The Sonic Society*. Accessed August 30, 2021. https://sonicsociety.org/who-is-jack-ward-in-the-audio-drama-world-anyway.

Wieland, Patience "Sibby." "A Brief History of Audio Drama." *Medium*. Accessed October 26, 2021. https://medium.com/acast/a-brief-history-of-audio-drama-5523475213f9.

Wikipedia. "The Mercury Theatre on the Air" entry. Accessed June 14, 2022. https://en.wikipedia.org/wiki/The_Mercury_Theatre_on_the_Air#Episodes.

———. Wikipedia's "ZBS Foundation" entry. Accessed August 30, 2021. https://en.wikipedia.org/wiki/ZBS_Foundation.

Wolinksy, David. Untitled interview with Jack Ward. *Don't Die*. Accessed November 12, 2021. https://nodontdie.com/jack-ward.

"ZBS Brings Back Radio Drama." *Bluefield Daily Telegraph* (November 23, 1978), A5.

Interviews

David Benedict (technician, writer, producer, actor, Atlanta Radio Theatre Company), interview with author, September 1, 2021.

Fred Greenhalgh (writer, director, producer, Dagaz Media), interview with author, August 30, 2021.

Jack Ward (producer, writer, host, The Sonic Society), interview with author, August 30, 2021.

Jeffrey Adams (producer, Icebox Radio Theater), interview with author, September 20, 2021.

Jerry Robbins (co-founder, artistic director, writer, Colonial Radio Theatre on the Air), interview with author, September 30, 2021.

Jim Wicker (literary manager, actor, The Radio Theatre Project) interview with author, September 21, 2021.

Joseph C. McGuire (producer, writer, Radio Theater Project), interview with author, August 31, 2021.

Lawrence Albert (founder and producer, Aural Vision, LLC.), interview with author, August 31, 2021.

M.J. Elliott (writer, Aural Vision, LLC.), interview with author, September 1, 2021.

Monica Sullivan (producer, Shoestring Radio Theatre), interview with author, October 6, 2021.

Robert Arnold (producer, writer, Spoken Signal Audio Drama), interview with author, September 14, 2021.

Roger Rittner (producer, Pulp Radio), interview with author, October 11, 2021.

Ron Butler (writer, Atlanta Radio Theatre Company), interview with author, September 29, 2021.

Steve Rubenstein (co-producer, Shoestring Radio Theatre), interview with author, October 6, 2021.

Thomas Lopez (producer, writer, ZBS Foundation), interview with author, September 1, 2021, September 2, 2021.

William Alan Ritch (president, Atlanta Radio Theatre Company), interview with author, October 8, 2021.

Index

Page references for charts are italicized.